GRAHAM FISHER MBE

IN MY OPINION

ESSAYS AND COMMENT ON
CONTEMPORARY SOCIAL ISSUES

with a foreword by

Zyllah Moranne-Brown

Marketing & Communications Director
Black Country Radio

SPARROW PUBLISHING

First published in UK by Sparrow Publishing 2021
Drovers Barn
Whitney-on-Wye
Herefordshire HR3 6EU

ISBN 978-0-7399212-0-0

Printed and bound in UK by print2demand.co.uk

By the same author:

Tales from the Barn (Sparrow Publishing 2019)
Jewels on the Cut (2nd edition) (Sparrow Publishing 2017)
Whiskers on Kittens (Sparrow Publishing 2015)
GlassCuts@50 (Sparrow Publishing 2014)
In Our Time (Sparrow Publishing 2013)
The 2012 Portland Vase Project (Sparrow Publishing 2012)
Jewels on the Cut (1st edition) (Sparrow Publishing 2010)
Playing the Game (Sparrow Publishing 2010)
Out of the Chair (Sparrow Publishing, 2009)
The Sweet Life (Sparrow Publishing, 2004)

DEDICATION

In recognition of her tireless commitment, professionalism and support in just about everything I take on, and for her even more remarkable tolerance in choosing to share her life with me, this one just has to be for Mary, or Spug – it's Scottish for 'little sparrow' – who also happens to be my publisher.

And for Mrs Chipmunk, as my dear mother Sheila is affectionately known. I think she would be the first to admit that her little lad didn't do too bad after all.

It follows logically that none of this would have been possible without either of them. So now all I have to do is fathom how I should ever have been so blessed by the Good Lord to share both in the one lifetime.

Spug   *Chipmunk*

ABOUT THE AUTHOR

Graham Fisher is a writer and broadcaster specialising in inland waterways and with an interest in the glass industries they served. Over many years he has carved a niche as an observer of the unusual or arcane which is reflected in his esoteric style. In 2001 he was invested with an MBE and in 2005 was voted by his peers as Inland Waterways Personality of the Year, assuming the mantle from previous recipients including John Craven OBE, David Suchet CBE and Timothy West CBE. In 2011 he was appointed to the West Midlands Waterways Partnership, part of the newly-formed Canal & River Trust, where he served with distinction. He has appeared on the public speaking circuit since an early age and has latterly become acknowledged as an ad hoc ambassador for the Stourbridge Glass industry. In 2015 he sat as a jury member for the International Festival of Glass Biennale. Shortly prior to the publication of this book in 2021 he was appointed a Fellow of the Royal Geographical Society (with IBG) in recognition of his work on the Midlands inland waterways network and the Stourbridge Glass industry together with his wider involvement in social, environmental and educational matters over many years in both the professional and voluntary sectors.

Yet alongside the numerous diverse avenues Graham has pursued in an eclectic career, central to his life has always been a love of radio.

His interest was inherited from his enthusiast father, who bought him his first 'transistor' and he vividly recalls precisely where he was on 22nd November 1963 when, as a nine-year old, he heard that JFK, the President of the USA, had been assassinated. By the 1990s he was a book reviewer for a local radio station and this led to the first in a series of his own shows.

Graham was subsequently invited to join the fledgling 102.5 The 'Bridge, now Black Country Radio, where he presented around the schedule including the flagship Breakfast Show. He was appointed Chairman of Stourbridge Radio Group Ltd and steered the station through its initial phase of establishing its footprint as the premier broadcasting outlet for the area.

He also has numerous television credits including appearances alongside Julia Bradbury (*Countryfile*), Johnny Vaughan (*Mud Men*), Alistair Appleton (*Escape to the Country*), and John Sergeant (*Barging Round Britain*).

In 2013 he relocated to the Welsh borderlands, which curtailed his 'live' broadcasts so he turned his attentions to podcasting and pre-recorded shows. In 2018 he was recognised in the Dudley Council for Voluntary Service Awards for his contribution to broadcasting. He continues to make regular contributions to Black Country Radio **www.blackcountryradio.co.uk** and is 'the voice of the Black Country' for West Midlands History **www.historywm.com**.

FOREWORD

I'm very fortunate to know Graham and have had the opportunity to spend numerous hours musing (yes, even as he cycles his way through Wales – a quick pit-stop phone chat in the middle of a field) and know he is indeed a man of many talents. A vast wealth of historic knowledge; just a brief chat takes you into the realms of Black Country history, intertwined memories and stories. He has the ability to tell a tale – to transfix with words both spoken and written. And an ability to connect with the soft Black Country dialect in both his words and his speech. Graham may now reside in the Welsh Borders but his true heart remains in the Black Country.

With multiple accolades, one more (and quite rightly) he has recently been recognised as a Fellow of the Royal Geographical Society (with IBG) in recognition of his work with the Society on the Midlands inland waterways network and the Stourbridge Glass industry, together with his wider involvement in social, environmental and educational matters over many years in both the professional and voluntary sectors.

Graham has been involved with local broadcasting and radio for many years and we are delighted that he still loves to contribute and work with Black Country Radio. He's always a delight to work with, and we've loved working with Graham as he develops his talents into the realms of podcasting; still a relatively new audio method but one that is becoming ever increasingly popular and maybe even more so, as the world is stuck at home.

So this new work *In My Opinion, Essays and Comment on Contemporary Social Issues* takes us on a journey of reflection on the strange world we now live in but in true style, questions a wide and diverse range of topics. From history, philosophy, science, religion, politics and much more Graham reflects on where we were and where we are, in his usual insightful and though-provoking analysis always mixed with wit and humour. Originally produced as a series of podcasts available on Black Country Radio's website (and wherever you get your podcasts from) these twenty chapters each have a cryptic title to draw in the reader (or listener as the case may be).

They demonstrate the pure joy and creative talent of Graham – writer, broadcaster, historian, thought provoker. And at this time, when the world is struggling with a pandemic we thought we could only see in Hollywood blockbusters, when our social interaction, cultural change and future opportunities and challenges are yet to restart, Graham's musings are more than relevant and thought provoking.

Zyllah Moranne-Brown
Marketing & Communications Director
Black Country Radio

WELCOME

Hallo, and thank you for browsing *In My Opinion.* Before delving any further I felt a brief explanation of what it's all about may prove helpful …

For various reasons, but largely attributable to zoning and a general tightening up on what is accessible on the internet, the way forward in the world of radio for the foreseeable future is via the podcast. This is *per se* quite remarkable when one considers the term didn't even exist just a few years back.

Rather fortuitously, and entirely coincidentally, I was recording a body of podcasts for my website when my colleagues at Black Country Radio kindly invited me to contribute to theirs. I presented *Tales from the Barn,* a collection of features which subsequently formed the basis for the book of the same name, published in 2019.

As *Tales from the Barn* was completing the publication stage, I began compiling a series of unrelated op-ed (opinions and editorials) contributions that I also submitted to BCR aimed at provoking thought and generating discussion.

Thus was born *In My Opinion* tagged as 'an occasional series of essays on themes on which writer and broadcaster Graham Fisher offers a personal view'. Random and subjective but – I like to think – balanced, they are entirely my own observations and I emphasise that their airing on Black Country Radio does not suggest or imply that they represent the opinion of the station. Or anyone else, for that matter.

Each episode of typically twelve minutes or so was independently written, narrated and produced by me from my base on the Welsh border. So, as we say in the Black Country, they are *'all me own werk'.* They were recorded between June 2019 and December 2020 and originally posted online at **www.blackcountryradio.co.uk** immediately thereafter.

Inevitably, events have moved on in the interim and so all have been supplemented by a Postscript of information that has since come to notice and which brings them as up to date as is practicable at the time of publication. The modified recordings can be heard at **www.grahamfisher.co.uk**

You might or might not agree with what is said, but I guarantee they will give food for thought. And that can't be a bad thing.

I am grateful to Black Country Radio and especially to Zyllah Moranne-Brown, Marketing & Communications Director, for her support and encouragement in airing the podcasts and for also graciously providing the Foreword to this book.

'Turn on, tune in, drop out'. (Timothy Leary 1920-1996, once described by President Richard Nixon as 'the most dangerous man in America'. Leary insisted 'drop out' was an innocuous metaphor for 'change.')

Graham Fisher
April 2021

CONTENTS

IN MY OPINION – the podcasts

Each episode is given a cryptic headline title of three words together with a brief description indicating its root theme, i.e. history, philosophy, science, religion, politics, *etc*. They are reproduced here as they appeared in the original podcasts.

A CLASS ACT   p11
Racism, feminism, ageism; are the 'isms' of our contemporary times still quietly but assuredly overshadowed by one of the oldest biases of all – the class structure?

GUILT BY DEGREE   p17
In simplistic terms, right is right and wrong is wrong. But in identifying transgressors let us continue to exercise our sense of proportion.

ART OR SCIENCE   p23
Did a mathematician born in the twelfth century unwittingly hold the key to our greater comprehension and practice of high art?

OFF THE WALL   p29
Nutters, fruit loops and basket cases are just some of the more derogatory and pejorative terms often levelled at those who march to the beat of a different drum. But, harmless as many of them may be in the pursuit of their own lives on their terms, do we belittle the true eccentric at our peril?

CRIME AND STATISTICS   p35
Whilst the doom-mongers and soothsayers may suggest we are all heading towards hell-in-a-handcart, this alternative examination of the 'evidence' may offer pause for reflection.

FLAT OR ROUND   p41
Well, is the earth flat or is it round? Or do we in fact live on the inside of the globe (if it is a globe) rather than the outside? In the State of Ohio, at least, it looks like your views and your rights to express them – however 'off the wall' they may be – are about to be enshrined in law.

PEAS AND QUEUES   p47
Our language is constantly evolving yet although this is inevitable are there some changes that, in the interests of accurate communication, we should resist? The apostrophe is dead; long live the apostrophe. But does it matter, and should we care?

HEAT AND LIGHT p53
Our insatiable thirst for energy is countered by increasing levels of atmospheric greenhouse gases and the imperative to tackle global warming. But do the established laws of science indicate that, ultimately, our fate may not lie entirely in our hands?

AGE OF REASON p59
A long-defunct grammar school, a pupil in the 'shallow waters' of his formative years and a celebration of half a century since the death of one of our greatest intellects, Graham reflects on how this rich combination may have inadvertently led to unintended consequences.

BEHIND THE BARRICADES p65
The coronavirus pandemic is of worldwide concern as the race is on to reduce transmission and develop a vaccine. Yet beyond the medical concerns, what implications are there for the eventual resumption of our 'normal' way of life and even upon the state of our democracy?

THOUGHTS ON THOUGHTS p71
As civil unrest and protests sweep across a world still reeling from the coronavirus pandemic, inequality and suppression are feeding a mood for change. GF ponders whether philosophy may offer a path towards a more level playing field on which that change may be grounded.

PAGES OF TIME p77
It is said that time moves in mysterious ways; according to Einstein it can even move at different speeds. But how exactly does it move? And does an appreciation of the philosophy of the motion of time offer an insight into conflict resolution? GF explores this from the perspective of *Books and Bookmen*, children's television and the after-shocks of a pandemic.

WALKING THE WALK p83
In a variation of the eternal nature-nurture debate, whether determined by personal preference or genetic disposition, we all have our own direction of travel through life. No two paths are the same and some are not so smooth as others, but perhaps there may be a utopian option that may help us all attain the same destination of communal harmony. GF explores the options.

MAD OR BAD? p89
Health and safety, a cornerstone of modern industrial practice since 1974, still attracts more than its fair share of ridicule. But is its denigration justified, and on what evidence do its detractors base their belittlement? GF takes a look from the perspective of a novel accolade.

A BETTER WAY
p95

Can scientific advancements trump good old-fashioned human knowledge and experience? GF examines the issue from the perspective of an appreciation of *Uisge Beatha*, the Gaelic 'water of life'.

ADMIRING THE VIEW
p101

Ever since Darwin's revolutionary notions on the origins of species, theories of evolution have been used to explain our natural world based on empirical principles. But do they always prove convincing beyond doubt over a more divine authority? GF examines issues of science *versus* faith based on his own personal quest for answers.

NEGATIVE TO POSITIVE
p107

As self-styled 'spiritual pilgrim' Beth Bruno declares: 'When we judge others, we dim our own light. And the world needs more light right now.' But how and why do we judge others on that scantest of information provided by initial appearances. And is that venerable adage 'you only get one chance to make a first impression' still relevant in the age of social media?

COLOURS OF POWER
p113

Rousing, rebellious, rumbustious; contentious combative and compelling. The USA Presidential Elections of 2020 have redefined politics in an unprecedented polarisation of opinion that may have ramifications way beyond the Land of The Free. But have they also sent us on a path that may change the course of democracy as we know it? And can we apply the brakes?

IN LOVING MEMORY
p121

Within a few years the internal combustion engine, arguably the most ubiquitous and liberating mechanical contraption ever invented, is to be outlawed in new cars and will be consigned to the history books. GF offers an affectionate reflection on what will be the end of an era.

ONE SMALL WORD
p127

In this intimate reflection GF takes an sideways look at Christmas by focussing on the usage and interpretation of just one associated word that, though comprising only two consonants and two vowels, has ramifications that extend way beyond Christianity and the festive season.

LAST WORD
p132

EPILOGUE
p133

*John Cleese, Ronnie Barker and Ronnie Corbett in the
'Class System' sketch from 1966 Frost Report*

A CLASS ACT

Racism, feminism, ageism; are the 'isms' of our contemporary times still quietly but assuredly overshadowed by one of the oldest biases of all – the class structure?

Some years ago in my days with what was then 102.5 The 'Bridge before its reincarnation as Black Country Radio, I ran an afternoon chat show in which a wide range of the great and the good extended me the courtesy of sitting opposite in the hot seat.

From Holy men to engineers, charity founders to entertainers, we welcomed the lot. One such was a local comedienne – am I allowed to employ that gender-specific term these days? Ah how times change but its use does narrow it down a bit as to whom I refer – anyway, a local comedienne who caused such uproarious merriment that saw me actually slide off my seat under the table in uncontrollable laughter whilst, in the next studio and ostensibly being introduced to the finer points of broadcasting, a gaggle of visitors looking through the window were themselves doubled up with laughter looking at me, doubled up with laughter. And the topic? My guest's ranting, excoriating diatribe on the difference between us Black Country Yam Yams and our neighbours across the cultural divide (beyond here be dragons) in Birmingham. Real knockabout stuff and very, very funny in its mock deprecation of both.

Though our sense of rivalry is of its own time and area we are not alone and there are numerous other examples of such parochial – and largely, though not always, similarly benign – antagonism across the land. In my student days at Sunderland many years ago I quickly learnt the difference between Wearsiders and their neighbouring Geordies, both of whom, to the outsider, apparently spoke the same language. Note to self and my Brummie mates; they think we talk the same, *doh you just 'ate that?* Thus do Yam Yams and Brummies coexist by continuing to hone their mutually disparaging but ultimately non-malevolent repertoire.

But imagine, for a moment, the nomenclatures are changed to, let's say, Tutsi and Hutu. The Rwandan genocide was a mass slaughter of Tutsi and moderate Hutu during the Rwandan Civil War of 1994. Up to one million Rwandans were killed, about 70% of the Tutsi population, and only ended with the military victory of the Rwandan Patriotic Front.

Closer to home but further back in history, the UK was the unwitting beneficiary of the dreadful religious persecution that lead to an influx of Huguenots who brought with them their skills including weaving, lacemaking and, particularly germane to the Stourbridge area, glassmaking. We could similarly examine the opposing factions in

Recorded 6 June 2019

the Irish troubles, much of the Middle East and many other parts of the globe. Now throw into this mix the potential for strife induced by differences in skin colour, lifestyle choice, sexual orientation or any other number of mutually incompatible factors that are politically *de rigeur* at the time and we have a potent mix for the stirring of malcontent.

All of these have two features in common. First, the problems as loosely described here are universally recognised. I guarantee I could count on the fingers of one hand the number of listeners who have not heard of – or even experienced for themselves – at least one. Second, at any given stage and depending upon their prominence within a given political cycle, huge amounts of effort, perhaps by way of social intervention, education or straightforward cash injections, are directed their way. Particularly, it seems, at election-time. Or is that just the cynic in me baring its fangs?

Yet there is one problem that still goes largely unreported, even unnoticed, certainly to the extent that little is actively done to address it. With a recognition factor that is inversely proportional to its capacity for destruction, it is a problem that has the potential to devastate society yet in a quietly malignant way that may find us wanting when it is too late to address by the standard fall-back methods we currently throw as we would lob a life-belt.

I'll name the problem in one word in just a moment, but before I do let me set the scene with the entirely true tale of a pub I frequented with my dear late father when we lived in Wollaston near Stourbridge back in the 1980s. It's an Indian Restaurant now, which is sad … not because it's an Indian Restaurant, and a rather good one at that, but because of what was lost in the transition.

You see, every Friday night my father and I would go there about 7pm, to be greeted by an already packed house that typically included a range of characters I will attempt to describe. At the bar were a group of friends who, having worked hard all week, intended to play hard for the weekend, commencing with a few beers in their local whilst attired in fancy dress of the day. One week they would be American cowboys, the next a gaggle of Regency fops, one never knew. At the far end of the bar, out of harm's way, were a group of workers in overalls that told their immediate past history prior to their wearers relaxing by competing over a game of darts.

In the lounge area to our left would be dinner-suited gents and coiffured ladies awaiting taxis to take them to the City for the evening – Birmingham, in those days, Wolverhampton was yet to achieve the status – whilst in the back room might be a group of men, inevitably men, of West Indian origin playing their unique variation of overarm dominoes … and so on, but I think you get the picture.

The point is, here was a microcosm of a representative, though not exhaustive, range of backgrounds, a cake slice through the gateaux of social strata, all mingling in *bonhomie.* The one thing that was not in any evidence whatsoever was that problem of one name I referred to earlier – class.

The class structure. That time-served feature of our lives that some would suggest has been the bedrock of our version of civilisation almost since these islands were first populated. Institutionalised and ingrained to the extent that it is taken as the norm moreso that its relevance to life in the twenty-first century is questioned, it is the glue that holds together the fabric of our social structure. But does it? Has the concept of class outgrown its usefulness to the extent that it may be damaging that which it seeks to protect?

Embedded in the class structure still lies the notion of imperialism. A century since the foundations of the British Empire began to crumble, many of our institutions and aspects of our educational system are still geared to providing skills and leaders for an entity that no longer exists. Change has been afoot for decades, the move from grammar schools towards a comprehensive education system being a notable manifestation, but in this context the general pace of such change has been anaemic. In the meantime, the breaking down of arbitrary barriers, particularly the rise of feminism, disability empowerment and equal rights, has created a dichotomy where the established order is no longer fit for purpose.

This is on a societal scale but a poignant example of it that hits home was provided by a thinker from amongst our own ranks. Former MP and broadcaster Brian Walden, born in West Bromwich and the son of a glassmaker had, prior to his death in May 2019, spent much of his life questioning the *status quo*. He told the simple but compelling tale – I would not be surprised if it were based on his own experience – of the factory operative, a working class man as he describes, who studied, gained proficiency and achieved promotion but who could never elevate himself past a certain level as others passed him by. He wondered why until his suspicions were confirmed one day when the wealthy owner put his arm around his shoulder and congratulated him on a good morning's work. 'Now' said the owner, 'I'll go for my lunch and you can get your dinner.'

If true, and it certainly rings as such, this represents an appalling indictment on the pernicious effects of the sliding scale of class. It lurks silently in the shadows, largely unnoticed or ignored by disinterested onlookers passing by on the other side and upon whom it has no effect, but by definition afflicts in increasing degrees those who fall lower down the order. Yet, whilst piecemeal strikes from the wings may have limited impact, there are no armies of social equalisers on the horizon preparing to cordon it off. Is it any wonder that people feel increasingly disenfranchised from those tasked with sourcing a resolution, in plotting a path forward?

And is this not being reflected in political upheavals, not just here but across Europe, that see a swing away from the established parties towards those offering alternatives, some of which may be attractive when clutching for straws but which are far from healthy under scrutiny in the longer term.

This is powerful stuff. And it should be of serious concern. Whereas not so long ago this reliance on one's background would, particularly in the days of Empire and a more general attitude of accepted servility, have been accepted as the inevitable if somewhat occasionally uncomfortable norm, society itself has moved on whilst those same norms have remained hidebound.

The growth in diversity, with all that entails in terms of broadening our communal perspectives, the explosion in education and the expectations arising therefrom, the recognition of alternate way of lifestyle, the rise in alternate social *mores* and perhaps most significantly, the profound shift in our country's role in a greater Europe and the world – in contrast with a time not so long ago when the sun never set on those parts we actually administered – all of these are at odds with a social scaffold fundamentally out of kilter with that it is intended to support. The long-term effect of this is at very least a weakening of the edifice. I will proffer no firmer prognosis because it is simply too traumatic to imagine the consequences of total collapse.

Yet it is not all doom and gloom, for we already have the nub of the solution in our grasp. That solution lies, as it inevitably must, in mutual respect and forbearance based on meritocracy, social mobility, inter-personal communications – anything, just anything other than outmoded social ideals based around accidents of birth.

And the result? Well, I give you exhibit a) in the form of that once-delightful pub in Wollaston. And, to demonstrate how this works on a larger scale, I present the utterly compelling exhibit b), namely us Black Country folk and them there Brummies.

Long may our feigned rivalry but ultimately generous cohabitation continue to offer the world a model of how, and in the best of humour, it can be achieved.

POSTSCRIPT

This from *Private Eye* magazine, issue 1525 of July 2020, *Letters to the Editor*, contributor Mr Anthony Dunn.

Sir,
While I welcome Slicker's quantitative exposure of 'PR platitudes' on Black Lives Matter *(Slicker being the pseudonym for the magazine's City correspondent – author)*, there is a massive elephant in his room. Not to mention, or better still, factor in class would probably have enlightened us much further.

Whilst there's no doubt many grandchildren of former East End barrow boys and market traders now flood into the City from Essex on the daily commute, I wonder how many of these end up in the boardroom? Likewise, how many from working and lower-middle-class stock are called to the Bar or become Doctors?

We do know, for example, that white, working class boys are the highest under-achievers in terms of education, whilst Oxbridge and Russell Group Universities, politics, medicine and law, for example, are over-represented by those from public schools and wealthy backgrounds. Mentioning race without class seems to be gaining currency without scrutiny, along with the idea that the UK's racial history seamlessly aligns with that of the US. It does not. With Orwellian alarm, I note that we are increasingly falling into the trap set by infantile identitarian politics.

Often well-meaning people balk at the class factor but if it is not present in these contexts I fear we will never get to the bottom of it, let alone a more equal society.

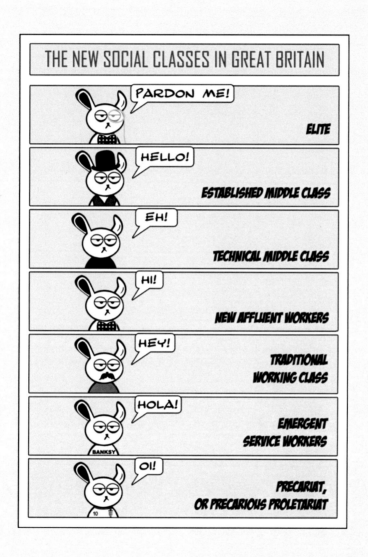

The Bracton treatise, created 1272–1307, composed in the wake of Magna Carta, is the most ambitious legal work from medieval England.

GUILT BY DEGREE

In simplistic terms, right is right and wrong is wrong. But in identifying transgressors let us continue to exercise our sense of proportion.

The foundations of laws of the United Kingdom are framed on precedents and *mores* stretching back for hundreds of years in a contiguous pedigree unrivalled in any other part of the Western world. Consequently, with such a history in the practise of fine-tuning, English law is almost universally unequivocal. By this I mean that, barring the occasional notable exception that usually follows a knee-jerk reaction in the 'something must be done' faculty of legislature – look no further than the reprehensible Guard Dogs Act of 1975, since largely amended – UK criminal law is clear, unambiguous and – crucially – quite absolute. Consider, for example, the law on theft as described in the Theft Act 1968 arguably one of the most effective pieces of legal drafting in the post-war era that, though subsequently amended, still has this definition in Section 1 (1) at its core:

'A person is guilty of theft if he dishonestly appropriates property belonging to another with the intention to permanently deprive the other of it.'

That is just beautiful. No argument. Simple, concise, unconditional and devoid of the taxing minutiae that bedevil philosophers in deliberating how many angels can dance on the head of a pin. But therein lies the paradox in its absolutism. Dishonestly appropriate a battleship or a biro, it is still theft and there is no accommodation in the definition for the magnitude of the acquisition, let alone the context or the *means rea*, i.e. the intention or knowledge of the perpetrator that then evokes questions of personal circumstances and mental state at the time of the offence.

Fortuitously, entwined throughout the legal system are the checks and balances that mitigate over-zealous interpretation of statutes or the common law. The enviable tradition of trial by Jury has its roots in Anglo Saxon England and the establishment of the magistracy dates back to The Justice of the Peace Act of 1361, many of the provisions of which are still in force today. Standing accused in front of one's fellow man – or woman; females were first allowed on juries in 1920 – affords judgement within the paradigm of 'honest and reasonable belief' in strict liability cases and the taking into account of mitigations and defence. Whilst not unique in this regard, the UK is up there in best practice. Conversely the assiduously unyielding observance of every dot and full stop is a prerequisite to a totalitarian state. We don't do that.

Thus has the law matured over the centuries, millennia even, into what we now take for granted as the cornerstone of a democratic law-respecting society. However, and mindful that rushed law is inevitably bad law with all that entails for civic respect of it – I detect a shift in this exemplar away from our time-served protocols and in a way that though well intentioned may ultimately not bode well unless that historical balance is maintained.

And I lay the cause at the feet of a trend that coincidentally or otherwise has seemed to proliferate commensurate with the prevalence of social media and its propensity to disseminate passion and subjectivity long before reason and objectivity have had time to strap their boots on, and that is the unfettered exposure and corrosive prosecution of the 'ism'.

There is a correlation here with the medical world, where the suffix 'itis' – which simply means 'inflammation' – can be appended to just about anything to describe a generic condition pertaining to the prefix, for example appendicitis, or inflammation of the appendix, similarly arthritis, gastritis, fibrositis and so forth.

Similarly the suffix 'ism' can be applied to elucidate a syndrome, or a collation of signs and symptoms that are correlated with each other in a particular point of reference as described by the prefix. Some are munificent or benign conditions, hence altruism, philanthropism. Others may be more provocative, either to a positive or negative extent depending on the perspective of the proponent, to whit, feminism, chauvinism, antisemitism – ah, that one seems to merit a chapter all of its own – ageism, sexism, despotism, fundamentalism … and the granddaddy of them all … racism.

A perpetual thorn in the pan-societal rump that varies in its discomfiture depending on which side one sits but which, despite occasional relief by shuffling around never seems to completely go away, and a topic that rouses emotions well above its weight even at the mention of its name, this exceptionally pernicious 'ism' is defined by the Oxford English Dictionary as: *Prejudice, discrimination, or antagonism directed against someone of a different race based on the belief that one's own race is superior.*

Gosh, even the taciturn description of the condition cries out for an emollient to soothe the unease; little wonder its practical application can realise such devastating consequences. Yes indeed, the OED definition is textually elegant in being unequivocal and absolute. But I contend that, just as with our definition of theft, which is trite in a comparison of *gravitas* but nonetheless amply makes the point regarding their mutual clarity, it must be interpreted within the round. This is not to dilute that interpretation, but to aid the mix to the desired strength in a holistic solution of minimal toxicity. Now that's not the sort of sentence that one should leave unattended for too long so I think I'd better explain my reasoning behind it.

Let's start with Idi Amin, a Ugandan military officer who served as President from 1971 to 1979. Being popularly known as the 'Butcher of Uganda' probably says it all about this particularly abominable psychopath; he is considered one of the most brutal despots in world history and his rule was characterised by rampant human rights abuses, political repression, ethnic persecution, extrajudicial killings, nepotism, corruption and gross economic mismanagement. International observers estimate that up to half a million people were killed under his regime. Now *that's* a top-of-the-range racist at the peak of his game.

Then there's the equally charming Robert Mugabe. Having dominated Zimbabwe's politics for nearly four decades he stands accused of being a dictator responsible for economic mismanagement, corruption, anti-white racism, human rights violations and crimes against humanity.

And finally in this *trio diabolique* I give you ... Adolf Hitler. What more need one say? Historian Ian Kershaw neatly sums up this ultra-egotistical maniac in one coruscating sentence: 'never in history has such ruination – physical and moral – been associated with the name of one man'.

Sadly, the list goes on, engulfing at varying times huge swathes of humanity under its scope of malevolence ... Joseph Stalin, Mao Zedong, Pol Pot, Eugene Terre Blanche. At a local level we can cite the killers of Stephen Lawrence as representative of a sad litany of ethnically motivated serious crimes that are now endemic in many of our major cities. Racists, every man-jack of them, and all fitting squarely into our definition.

Now compare and contrast these with the example from March 2019 of a BBC interview in which white politician Amber Rudd referred to black politician Dianne Abbott as 'coloured'. Notwithstanding the former was being supportive of the latter in sympathising with her treatment on social media and elsewhere – which, *per se*, is patently offensive – the use of that one word sparked Twitter-storms of controversy.

Abbot herself said: 'The term 'coloured' is an outdated, offensive and revealing choice of words.' (*Note to self* – revealing of what, exactly?) whilst Danielle Rowley, the Labour MP for Midlothian, helpfully tweeted: 'Amber Rudd undermining an important point about online abuse by referring to Diane Abbott as a 'coloured woman' on *@BBC Radio 2*. She clearly gets her language from the same bygone era as her abhorrent welfare policies.' Really?

The inferences were clear – in fact there are those who went beyond inference in ramping up the rhetoric to declare Rudd a blatant racist and, thanks to the miracles of technology, a hitherto essentially private spat was opened up for unencumbered comment across the planet from those who also felt offended by proxy on Ms Abbott's behalf. Rudd responded to the storm with a dignified apology. 'Mortified at my clumsy language and sorry to *@HackneyAbbott*' she tweeted. 'My point stands: that no one should suffer abuse because of their race or gender'. Quite right, though here is a fascinating fact courtesy of the Wikipedia school of philosophy; the term 'women of colour' surfaced in the USA in the violence against women movement. In the late seventies it unified all women experiencing multiple layers of marginalisation with race or ethnicity as a common issue.

Back in the 1960s I remember the first boy of West Indian descent to join our otherwise all-white infants school. They were interesting times as we adjusted to this strange newcomer, and *vice versa*. His name was Tony and we became good friends for a while until our paths parted on changing schools. It was all a very long time ago but I well recall how any signs of inappropriate conduct towards him were quickly defused by our teachers literally banging heads together – altogether now, all of those over a certain age who remember when teachers actually did that. Nowadays, of course, the expression is purely allegoric and anyone below state retirement age would not even appreciate the metaphor let alone its efficacy in modifying errant juvenile behaviour. How times change.

Sixty years later Amber Rudd committed the cardinal error of negotiating the hot embers of personal sensitivities whilst wearing hobnail boots instead of ballet shoes. Perhaps her comments were crass, insensitive – maybe, for someone who should be expected to have well-honed political antennae, even misguided or plain ignorant. But in denouncing her as racist are we truly comfortable in conflating this unfortunate episode with that same fire-breathing chimera of hatred and bigotry that begat the likes of Amin, Mugabe or Hitler?

Ah, thank goodness for those historic aspects of our legislature, the glues that bind us, that have over centuries become embedded in our cultural psyche and which allow us to identify the degrees of culpability and in turn avoid us treading the slippery slopes towards despotism. But in doing so we must also respect the delicacy of the dividing line. At the end of the day, steal a battleship or steal a biro; theft is theft and it is wrong. Racism is racism; that is wrong too and must be countered with that ultimate vigour with which we defend all of our values. Yet in apportioning to transgressors the appropriate measure of criticism, censure or punishment it will remain to our eternal credit as a society that we continue to exercise the judgement of degree.

The campaign "Is it racism?"
Generation 2.0 for Rights, Equality & Diversity –
a nonprofit organisation based in Athens,
"consisting of people with different origins who work
together to promote equal participation in a diverse
society, through the empowerment of communities."

POSTSCRIPT

In 2010 *The Race and Faith Inquiry* report said the term 'institutional racism' has become a barrier to reform at the Metropolitan Police and is 'a millstone around the neck'. The term was used by Sir William Macpherson in 1999 in his report into Stephen Lawrence's murder. The inquiry report says the phrase 'institutional racism' is used too glibly as a 'blanket indictment'.

In June 2020, following a ten-year investigation, a report on 'institutional racism' was released in which the author acknowledged the concept of ingrained bias but suggested that in many instances this was more a result of 'institutional ignorance or misunderstanding' rather than blatant racism.

BBC Online

The Statue of Justice atop the Central Criminal Court in Old Bailey, London

1 petal: Calla Lily

2 petals: Euphorbia

3 petals: Trillium

5 petals: Columbine

8 petals: Bloodroot

13 petals: Black-eyed Susan

21 petals: Shasta daisy

34 petals: Field daisies

ART OR SCIENCE

Did a mathematician born in the twelfth century unwittingly hold the key to our greater comprehension and practise of high art?

The following is merely an idea. I claim little intellectual rigour in its derivation but offer it as a catalyst for debate in the enduring quest to reconcile high art and pure science, a theme that has exercised me since the halcyon days of my youth. But it is my more recent induction into the world of glass that has revitalized my re-examining the connection from a sideways perspective; namely, the skills involved in glassmaking. For which, of course, Stourbridge is famous. However, *quod erat demonstrandum*, this same principle may equally apply to other skills requiring a combination of cognitive and psychomotor abilities for which the Black Country is long renowned.

A bold aim, but we cannot soar with the eagles on the wings of a wren. Allow me to get airborne ...

First, the key player.

It was Bertrand Russell who suggested that 'numbers hold sway above the flux of life'. Thus was it ever so and our hero of the moment is the Italian mathematician Fibonacci (c.1170–c.1250) who, like Russell, was one of the finest minds of his day. His book *Liber Abaci* examined a system of Hindu-Arabic numbering that featured the astonishing arrangement that came to be known by his name. It is said that he initially used the sequence to estimate the fastest rate at which rabbits could copulate but it proved to have far wider corollaries. Here it is ...

Fibonacci numbers comprise a progression beginning with 0 then 1 and followed by the addition of each succeeding number to its predecessor ie; 0, 1, 1 (0+1), 2 (1+1), 3 (2+1), 5 (3+2), 8 (5+3), 13 (8+5), and so forth *ad infinitum*. Remove the sums for clarity and the sequence reads: 0, 1, 1, 2, 3, 5, 8, 13, 21, 34, 55, 89, 144, 233, 377 ... *etcetera, etcetera*.

Et voilà, here's the magic. In nature the number of petals on many flowers is a Fibonacci number. There are numerous other instances of correlation to the extent that mathematician and philosopher Adolf Zeising (1810–1876) proposed it as a universal law of nature. But this is merely the beginning. If the larger number is divided by the one preceding it then, ignoring the first few until everything settles, the ratio steadies out at around 1.62. This has become known as the Golden Ratio, Golden Mean or Divine Proportion and even has its own mathematical symbol, the Greek letter *phi* (Φ).

The ratio has been shown to be 'psychologically pleasing' in that it is a natural ratio that the eye coordinates to the brain. Thus no surprise that its dimensions were deployed

Recorded 9 August 2019

extensively throughout the Renaissance and to this day artists and photographers still use a Fibonacci ratio as the most popular shape of canvas or image. Yet it would be interesting to hear how many would be willing to quantify why, other than 'it just looks right'.

And still the elegant beauty of the Fibonacci sequence unfurls. Take the lowest number and create a square of one unit, then place it adjacent to another of the same. Below these, place a 2-unit square then build up the squares *(Figure 1)*. The longer side of each square is the length of two successive Fibonaccis and each square has sides that are Fibonaccis. The *coup de grace*: describe a quarter circle in each of the squares *(Figure 2)* and behold; the shape of numerous *objets* that occur in nature, from nautilus shells to broccoli florets and even the human ear.

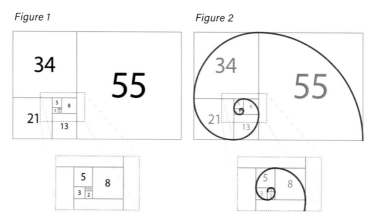

Figure 1   *Figure 2*

Fibonacci spirals in nature:

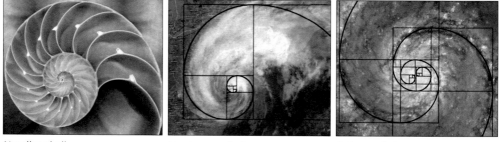

Nautilus shell   Hurricane spiral   Galaxy spiral

Now, let us hold this in abeyance as I turn to the 2012 Portland Vase Project, a magnificent initiative headed up by life-long glass-man Ian Dury to recreate this iconic piece of Roman cameo glass in Stourbridge. I was the official biographer for the venture and shadowed it throughout. Mere words are almost inadequate in capturing the sheer brilliance of master glassmaker Richard Golding as he started it all off by blowing the blanks but I gave it my best shot when I wrote:

'I was transfixed as, with an efficiency of movement and a deftness of touch that redefines sublime, he slowly, resolutely enticed that amorphous gobbet of semi-liquid into a masterpiece of exquisiteness that would feign serve the Gods themselves. This, Dear Reader, transcends mere talent; we were witnessing a gift that was nudging at the echelons of pure genius.'

Fast forward to May 2014 when I delivered a presentation on Stourbridge Glass in, of all places, Stourbridge.

Following my talk I was presented with a stunning glass bowl made by glass *artiste* Allister Malcolm. It sits in pride of place at home, next to a couple of tumblers that he presented to me on a previous occasion.

I was looking at them one morning when I wondered if the patterns on Allister's bowl could be a Fibonacci number. Intrigued, I annotated every dot and marking. And my findings?

Absolutely nothing. No correlation whatsoever.

I placed the bowl back next to the glasses and rued my fool's errand. Until that is, I took another look at the glasses. The image of Sherlock Holmes admonishing his chronicler 'You see, Watson, but you do not observe' punctuated my thoughts as I made closer inspection of something I had looked at a thousand times but failed to observe; the whorls in their bases resembled nautilus shells. Not exact, I confess, but near enough to rekindle my excitement as I scrabbled to find the telephone to ring Allister. The burning question on my mind: was this something he had done deliberately and knowingly or did it simply 'just look right?'

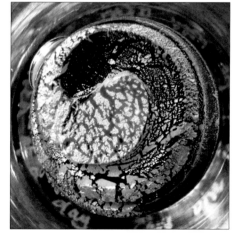

As the tone burr-burred I bet myself a tenner that Allister would humour me, courteously, as some sort of crank.

I lost.

It transpired that Allister had learnt about Fibonacci and the Golden Mean in his undergraduate days. It was not something he had particularly explored but he had found it a useful bookmark when ideas 'didn't quite look right' by dint of being outside of what he felt was 'pleasing proportions'. So, the acid question; was the shape in the base of his glasses deliberate or unplanned? 'I never gave it a thought' he told me. 'It's just how I made them … but now you come to mention it …'

The whorl within the tumbler base

I allude once more to Holmes when he remarks to Watson: 'Art in the blood is liable to take the strangest forms'. The quote is particularly prescient here since art surely takes no stranger form than the ability to manipulate a blob of molten silica into a thing of exquisite beauty. But, in what amounts to a slant on the classic nature-nurture conundrum, how much of this is 'a gift … nudging at the echelons of pure genius' or to what extent are such talents the consequence of a pragmatic rationale that is yet to be quantified?

And this is quintessence of my ruminations; if such talent is pragmatically quantifiable then it can be expressed as a strand of logic, represented by a mathematical function. That being the case it can be learnt. *Ergo*, if it can be learnt, *it can be taught*. Thus, by extraction, its teaching is not constrained by geography or timescale.

The implications of communicating across divides by means of prescription – and to store in retrieval systems for future generations – that which we presently consider to be almost divine are awesome. Yet the broader principle is a valid one that is already employed routinely in the teaching of cognitive skills. Consider, for example driving a motor vehicle:

The coordination in learning to control a car – ask any seventeen year-old – is a formidable undertaking. The task is made the more palatable by breaking down the action of, say, changing gear into a series of steps whereby each step is represented by a succession of the simplest elements to which the task can be reduced. Master each element in sequence then put them all together for the completed action.

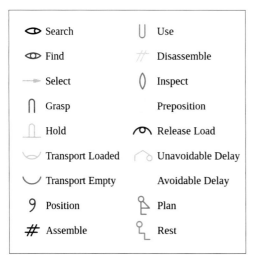

The basic motion elements or therbligs

Hey presto; a crossover between cognitive and psychomotor behaviour – the condensing of basic motion elements into a series of *therbligs*, thus named by Frank Bunker Gilbreth (1868–1924), a time-and-motion specialist who branded his brainchild by spelling his surname backwards.

Broadly analogous to therbligs in terms of function, *algorithms* were propounded in ancient times by Euclid of Alexandria but have been elevated in our consciousness more recently with the massive expansion in computer technology.

Quite simply, an algorithm is a step-by-step procedure for data processing and the somewhat sinister-sounding *automated reasoning* that proceeds through a number of defined steps until its objective is attained.

We are routinely subject to algorithms; accessing a bank account, online purchasing, social media – all are based on increasingly powerful algorithms that were the stuff of wild imaginings just a few years ago. *Moore's Law*, named after Gordon E Moore who founded the Intel ('Integrated Electronics') Corporation, postulates that computing power increases exponentially by doubling approximately every two years. It is thus a plausible *sequitur* to postulate that it is merely a matter of time before psychomotor skills may similarly be represented by a formula as a function of automated reasoning.

I contend it is not a question of if, but when, and that the period it may take should be considered an incentive more than a deterrent. The Higgs-Boson particle, identified courtesy of the Cern Large Hadron Collider, was but a fantastical notion in the mind of David Higgs for over forty years. Similarly, not quite there yet but getting ever closer, is the unifying 'theory of everything' that has exercised the likes of Steven Hawking for generations. Watch this space.

By these yardsticks the formulation of an encryption founded on the principle of Fibonacci that may be primal to glassmaking and other cognitive psychomotor abilities would appear to be relatively small beer. Its discovery may ultimately be by someone who has Isaac Newton's providence to see further than others by standing on the shoulders of giants and simply popping the final piece into the jigsaw.

Intriguing possibilities indeed, but lying across the path of our insatiable quest for pure logic I spy a Pandora's box that holds weighty issues of morality and ethics. Do we embrace such developments with the optimistic anticipation of Huxley's *Brave New World* or do we rebuff them in trepidation as a nightmarishly Orwellian analogy of *1984*? Ah, I see the cue to take my bow, for it will require far finer minds that mine to navigate through that one.

In the meantime, casting science aside I shall continue to frequent the Stourbridge Glass Quarter and marvel at these virtuosos, for surely that is what they are, plying their mesmerizing art in time-honoured fashion. Do join me there; I guarantee you will be impressed.

POSTSCRIPT

'Mathematician Vicky Neal explores the emotional, aesthetic and creative qualities that underpin the most beautiful maths … Nicholas Ross tells us how composers like Mozart have used mathematical ideas like the Golden Section and Fibonacci Sequence to structure their works. Does it really have an impact on the enjoyment of them?'

A Mathematician's Guide to Beauty BBC Radio 4, 21 February 2020.

OFF THE WALL

Nutters, fruit loops and basket cases are just some of the more derogatory and pejorative terms often levelled at those who march to the beat of a different drum. But, harmless as many of them may be in the pursuit of their own lives on their terms, do we belittle the true eccentric at our peril?

Right from the opening paragraphs of his glorious little tome *Great Eccentrics*, first published in 1984, author Peter Bushell escorts us, so we are informed, on 'a grand tour of the bizarre technicolour world of the eccentric' and mourns 'a world of increasing conformity in which individuality is being corroded almost daily' before celebrating the lives of such oddball luminaries as Squire Osbaldstone who defeated the French tennis champion using just his hand as a racquet, Jonas Hanway who was convinced that tea drinking was the root of all social evil leading to divorce and suicide, and Lt Col Alfred Daniel Wintle MC, described in his Daily Express obituary as 'a real corpse reviver who took more boredom out of life in the 1950s and 1960s than any other man in Britain'.

The unflattering but accurate *soubriquet* of 'Mad Jack Wintle' or 'Colonel Bogey' as he was known in the popular press, probably explains it all. He despised bureaucracy and his skirmishes with bloated authority became legendary. In 1966, as he predicted he would, he 'died of a clot'. Splendid stuff.

Indeed, as I compose this right now, I notice a similarly themed book *Eccentric Lives and Peculiar Notions* also first published in the same year as Bushell's and written by author and esotericist John Michell, in which he celebrates the extraordinary lives of, amongst others, Lady Blount and her efforts on the waters of the Old Bedford Level to prove the earth was flat, and Colonel Charles de Laet Waldo Sibthorp MP, the most conservative member of Parliament in history who opposed even the mildest amendment on any aspect of the historic English constitution. The gloriously bonkers Sibthorp denounced the Great Exhibition of 1851 as an alien plot and called upon God to smite the Crystal Palace with hailstones and lightning.

It may not be too hard to deduce from these representative residents of my bulging bookshelves, for which by dint of sheer space each candidate must fully justify its inclusion, that I have a sympathy and, since I am told – though I would vehemently disagree – that my own life is oft conducted within a parallel universe, a certain empathy with those to whom as Bushell suggests display their differences in their crotchets by marching to the beat of a different drum.

Recorded 26 September 2019

And, after being fascinated by such characters as Lord Monboddo, who was convinced that all babies were born with tails, and the scientist philosopher JBS Haldane – described by Nobel Laureate Sir Peter Medawar as 'the cleverest man I ever knew' – whose bleak but highly irreverent poem published in 1964 about his own terminal carcinoma has attained the status of minor masterpiece, I have concluded that whilst we may have issues in managing our great institutions such as the NHS, be floundering in the mire of our relations with our European neighbours or riven with social divisions seemingly unsolvable by our politicians, the one field in which we consistently float like cream to the top is in our unrelenting procreation of the Great British Nutcase. And long may it continue, for in the depths of adversity, sadness or strife are they not a source of comfort, perhaps inspiration for those of us trailing in their wake of weirdness who would at heart simply love to have the personal courage, inner conviction or sheer finger-waving defiance, to also march to that different drum beat; to do it, *à la Sinatra*, their way.

Other countries sustain their fair share of oddballs of course, but here in good ol' Blighty we can enjoy a particularly bounteous crop that punches well above its weight. They may not be eccentric all of the time or in all of their views; the distinguished Victorian scientist Francis Galton otherwise blotted his copybook with his proposal that only the upper classes should be allowed to breed. Conversely Dr William Price was a revolutionary Welsh Druid who geared his life according to his beliefs and routinely performed ceremonies at the 'serpent temple' in Wales erected by Druid revivalists. Then again, is Dr Price brought under the umbrella of eccentric simply by manifestation of his lifestyle and beliefs? Many modern-day followers of Druidism would doubtless dispute the suggestion.

Yes, it's a tricky one to nail down but etymology is always a helpful starting point so let's head there. Eccentricity is defined by the Oxford English Dictionary as the quality or habit of deviating from what is customary, and in engineering terms it also describes something that is off-centre. But this bland definition of the condition goes little way to defining what makes an eccentric, which takes us deep into the realms of psychology, the working of the brain, even the irreconcilable nature-nurture argument. Forgive me for not going there, for I am but a humble scribe; yet one aspect of which I am sure is that it is unnoticed by the sufferer, to whit, I am suggesting that it is a self effacing prophecy and that anyone who believes or states themselves to be eccentric is emphatically not.

Therein lies the leap from overt ostentation, gregariousness, extroversion or similar self-conscious characteristics that fall more accurately within the *oeuvre* of showmanship. The true eccentric, however bizarre the condition may manifest itself, would look agog upon anyone suggesting such a thing; the true eccentric believes their own views to be entirely mainstream, rational and normal. To suggest otherwise would rail the defence of the proud mom at her son's Army pass-out parade who declares proudly: 'Ooh look, Johnny is the only one in step'.

All simple enough in our not-too-academically rigorous examination of the term in this context, but probe much further and distinctions become decidedly blurred. And lest the examples already given here may create the impression that eccentrics are universally benign souls, a source of amusement and wonderment by their antics but hardly likely to ultimately threaten the fabric of society, we must clarify that this is not so. Eccentricity, or, harking back to the OED definition, the quality or habit of deviating from what is customary, can equally be a force for malevolence. Stand and be counted those to whom I routinely allude as representative of type simply because such is their unique behaviour that I need not detain you with an explanation of their vile accomplishments, the name alone is sufficient; Idi Amin, Robert Mugabe and the daddy of them all, A Hitler Esq. Genocidal maniacs? Not a word of it in their eyes and if it were possible to interview these and their colleagues in the hall of infamy – and not forgetting some females as well; there are those who would now include freedom doyenne Aung San Suu Kyi who has been deposed from her lofty perch following the alleged genocide of Rohingya Muslims – I fair guarantee they would all consider themselves entirely justified in their rationale despite being 'the only one in step'.

Which brings us to more pragmatic considerations of eccentric behaviour, especially when those eccentrics – who wouldn't ever describe themselves as such and would continue to entertain the clear misapprehension as to their own exemplary logic – may have ultimate control over the lives of thousands or even millions of people. The spectacular catalogue of verifiably nonconformist decisions of President Donald Trump – I make no political comment on whether they are right or wrong, but they are decidedly off the wall – continue to astound and cause jaws to drop in disbelieving awe. But he, and millions of his followers, consider him entirely reasonable. Should those who do not – and even those that do – be ever so slightly apprehensive that his index finger hovers over a big red button?

Closer to home we have the farrago – for that is what is – the jumbled mess of Brexit largely compounded by those of wildly disparate views, some of which by any pan-acceptable yardstick are nudging dangerously into the zones of extremity, and all by people who would argue to the end they are entirely reasonable and further claiming to act on behalf of their followers who think likewise.

I must question if there has been an explosion in the number of eccentrics that fall within our definition, or whether I have stretched that definition beyond its bubble of self-containment. It is certainly a far cry from our traditional acceptance of eccentricity as expounded by Nesta Webster who, throughout Britain in the 1920s, promulgated the idea that civilisation was threatened by an unholy combination of occultists and Freemasons. She was, in the classical sense, crackers. But ultimately innocuous. Not quite so our contemporary entourage, it seems. And there's the cause for unease; historical events may not repeat themselves but they do sometimes rhyme.

The Shavian alphabet, also known as the Shaw alphabet, was posthumously funded by and named after Irish playwright George Bernard Shaw. It was conceived as a way to provide simple, phonetic orthography to replace difficulties of conventional spelling.

One Shavian maxim that has passed into widespread usage states: 'The reasonable man adapts himself to the world: the unreasonable one persists in trying to adapt the world to himself. Therefore all progress depends on the unreasonable man.'

Reputedly one of the world's top leadership experts whose guidance is sought by the

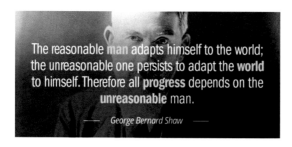

The reasonable man adapts himself to the world; the unreasonable one persists to adapt the **world** to himself. Therefore all **progress** depends on the **unreasonable** man.

—— *George Bernard Shaw* ——

likes of rock stars, royalty, politicians and business executives, Robin Sharma says:

'This is one of my favorite quotes from George Bernard Shaw. Sure, be practical. I agree it's important to use common sense. True, foolish risks can lead to difficult consequences. But having said that, don't be so scared of failure and disappointment that you fail to dream. Don't always be so reasonable and practical and sensible that you refuse to seize glorious opportunities when they show up and push the envelope as to what's possible for you. The world needs many more dreamers. Unreasonable souls who fight the urge to be ordinary. You can be one of them. Beginning today!'

In the blink of an eye, or within one paragraph at least, Mr Sharma seamlessly transgresses the line from erudite observation to not-too-subtle sales pitch and I understand the urban slang response to his closing entreaty runs along the lines of: 'yeah, right, whatever'.

Nevertheless, it would be enlightening to ascertain if many of our current movers and shakers have been influenced by Mr Sharma's work – frankly implausible – or, perhaps more likely by the entirely random nature of their chromosomes, are predisposed to move in that direction. Answers on a postcard, please.

Me? I'll just continue to listen to my heart whilst others discuss their soul but I will conclude with a provocative *bon mot* on eccentricity that is equally germane to our nonconformists as it is to engineering yet which has entirely distinct ramifications; it only takes one crank to start a revolution.

POSTSCRIPT

There is a rumour that the great American satirist (and gifted mathematician, as it happens) Tom Lehrer gave up political satire when the man held responsible for bombing Vietnam back to the stone age, Henry Kissinger, was awarded the Nobel Peace Prize in 1973. More accurately, Lehrer did comment that awarding the prize to Kissinger made political satire obsolete but denied that he stopped creating satire as a form of protest, pointing out that he had not toured for several years previously. But still, he made his point.

I feel a parallel creeping up behind me here and, in just two words, that parallel is Donald Trump. In suggesting that you, Dear Reader, do nothing more than check the man's record between the time of writing this podcast in September 2019 and the publication of this book, I need do nothing more than rest my case and, *à la Lehrer*, withdraw gracefully.

Shavian alphabet

𐑐	𐑚	𐑑	𐑛	𐑒	𐑜	𐑓	𐑝	𐑔
peep	**b**ib	**t**ot	**d**ead	**k**ick	**g**ag	**f**ee	**v**ow	**th**igh
[p]	[b]	[t]	[d]	[k]	[g]	[f]	[v]	[θ]
𐑕	𐑟	𐑖	𐑠	𐑗	𐑡	𐑘	𐑢	𐑙
so	**z**oo	**s**ure	mea**s**ure	**ch**urch	**j**udge	**y**ea	**w**oe	hu**ng**
[s]	[z]	[ʃ]	[ʒ]	[ʧ]	[ʤ]	[j]	[w]	[ŋ]
𐑤	𐑮	𐑥	𐑯	𐑦	𐑰	𐑧	𐑱	𐑨
loll	**r**oar	**m**ime	**n**un	**i**f	**ea**t	**e**gg	**a**ge	**a**sh
[l]	[r]	[m]	[n]	[ɪ]	[iː]	[e]	[eɪ]	[æ]
𐑩	𐑳	𐑪	𐑴	𐑫	𐑵	𐑬	𐑶	𐑭
ado	**u**p	**o**n	**oa**k	w**oo**l	**oo**ze	**ou**t	**oi**l	**ah**
[ə]	[ʌ]	[ɒ]	[əʊ]	[ʊ]	[uː]	[aʊ]	[ɔɪ]	[ɑː]
𐑸	𐑹	𐑺	𐑻	𐑼	𐑽	𐑾	𐑿	
are	**or**	**air**	**ur**ge	**arr**ay	**ear**	**ia**n	**yew**	
[ɑːr]	[ɔːr]	[ɛə]	[ɜːr]	[ər]	[ɪər]	[ɪə]	[juː]	

Abbreviations

𐑯	𐑓	𐑝	𐑞	𐑑
and	for	of	the	to

Sample text

𐑷𐑤 𐑣𐑿𐑥𐑩𐑯 𐑚𐑰𐑦𐑙𐑟 𐑸 𐑚𐑹𐑯 𐑓𐑮𐑰 𐑯 𐑰𐑒𐑢𐑩𐑤 𐑦𐑯 𐑛𐑦𐑜𐑯𐑦𐑑𐑰 𐑯
𐑮𐑲𐑑𐑕. 𐑞𐑱 𐑸 𐑧𐑯𐑛𐑬𐑛 𐑢𐑦𐑞 𐑮𐑰𐑟𐑯 𐑯 𐑒𐑪𐑯𐑖𐑩𐑯𐑕 𐑯 𐑖𐑫𐑛 𐑨𐑒𐑑
𐑑𐑩𐑢𐑹𐑛𐑟 𐑢𐑳𐑯 𐑩𐑯𐑳𐑞𐑼 𐑦𐑯 𐑩 𐑕𐑐𐑦𐑮𐑦𐑑 𐑝 𐑚𐑮𐑳𐑞𐑼𐑣𐑫𐑛.

All human beings are born free and equal in dignity and rights. They are endowed with reason and conscience and should act towards one another in a spirit of brotherhood.
(Article 1 of the Universal Declaration of Human Rights)

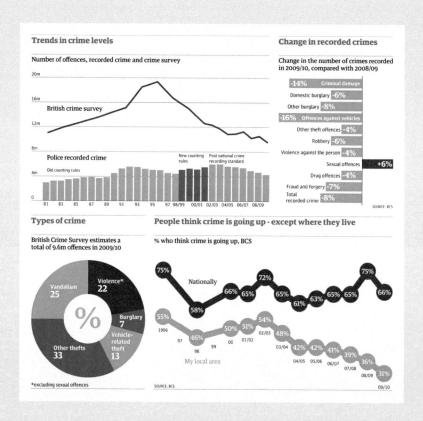

Trends in crime levels

Number of offences, recorded crime and crime survey

British crime survey

Police recorded crime

Old counting rules — New counting rules — Post national crime recording standard

81 83 85 87 89 91 93 95 97 98/99 00/01 02/03 04/05 06/07 08/09

Change in recorded crimes

Change in the number of crimes recorded in 2009/10, compared with 2008/09

-14%	Criminal damage
Domestic burglary	-6%
Other burglary	-8%
-16%	Offences against vehicles
Other theft offences	-4%
Robbery	-6%
Violence against the person	-4%
Sexual offences	+6%
Drug offences	-4%
Fraud and forgery	-7%
Total recorded crime	-8%

SOURCE: BCS

Types of crime

British Crime Survey estimates a total of 9.6m offences in 2009/10

Vandalism 25
Violence* 22
Burglary 7
Vehicle-related theft 13
Other thefts 33

%

*excluding sexual offences

People think crime is going up - except where they live

% who think crime is going up, BCS

Nationally: 75%, 58%, 66%, 65%, 72%, 65%, 61%, 63%, 65%, 65%, 75%, 66%

My local area: 55% (1996), 46% (97), 50% (00), 51% (01/02), 54% (02/03), 48% (03/04), 42% (04/05), 42% (05/06), 41% (06/07), 39% (07/08), 36% (08/09), 31% (09/10)

SOURCE: BCS

CRIME AND STATISTICS

Whilst the doom-mongers and soothsayers may suggest we are all heading towards hell-in-a-handcart, this alternative examination of the 'evidence' may offer pause for reflection.

A fundamental objective of reasoned debate is balance. But it is in the subjective identification of the centre of balance that, perversely, oft proves contentious. Whilst the ideal is for all opinions to be equally respected the facts of life dictate that it doesn't always work like that.

Two schools of thought illustrate the point. Let us first consider the apportioning of weight argument, in which the greater the bandwidth of disciples the more exposure it merits, and look no further than pre-election time when political groups are afforded media coverage commensurate with their size. Mainstream parties gorge the lion's share, smaller ones lag behind expectantly and no-hopers are noticeable by their absence.

Quod erat demonstrandum I present the fortunes of Screaming Lord Sutch and his Official Monster Raving Loony Party. I cannot recall ever seeing the man asserting his policies in a televised party-political broadcast, despite his ostensibly fruitcake suggestions for the lowering of the age of consent, passports for pets and numerous other ideas for which he was ridiculed at the time all having since, in some form or other, come to pass. Consider his fledgling Ministry For Rock and Roll alongside the contemporary Department for Digital, Culture, Media & Sport and we're one small step nearer to competently critiquing his prescience.

And, as Hamlet said, there's the rub; the impossibility of balancing current exposure against future outcomes. Even more perplexing are examples of incongruous views being marginalised by received wisdom whilst attracting populist support. Step forward Beppe Grillo, a professional comedian whose offensive jokes about politicians led to his television appearances being curtailed, albeit one aired in 1993 attracted 15 million viewers. Despite being branded by *Der Spiegel* magazine as 'the most dangerous man in Europe', he is hugely popular and in the 2018 Italian General Election his Five Star movement, of which he is a co-founder, became the largest individual party in Government.

The contrasting school of thought suggests that, when compared against the accepted paradigm, one's views may be universally considered dichotomous or extreme but should those views enjoy the longevity of consistent accuracy then credence should be afforded to them irrespective of the measure of their popular recognition. History is punctuated with examples of those who have steadfastly stood as a lone voice, marginalised and ignored, only to be ultimately proven correct. Winston Churchill, anyone?

Living without certainty is a burden under which we all toil particularly if the burden be the pursuit of truth. And how spurious a path that pursuit may take; the simpler the truth may appear, the greater the deceit. Consider the schoolboy inanity that suggests 'my dog has four legs; my cat has four legs, therefore my dog is a cat'. Now extend this into the equally facile proposition: 'if 25% of all road collisions are caused by intoxicated drivers then it must follow that 75% are caused by those who are sober. Therefore it is much safer to be drunk'. Which, of course, is utter nonsense.

Lest these sound just too silly for words they are in essence rooted in the principle of *reductio ad absurdum,* which as the name suggests, reduces logic to such a point where the conclusion becomes absurd, and which can be traced back many centuries to early Grecian scholars, notably Xenophanes, Plato, Socrates, Euclid and Archimedes. Its validity has been contemplated and refined ever since; in modern medicine it is the fundament for reducing the strength of a medication to the point at which it is no longer effective, thereby identifying the minimal viable dosage. Ah, suddenly the power of philosophical deliberation on existential realities becomes coherent, *et voilà*, things are no longer quite as absurd as they seem. Or are they?

As with any great revelation visited upon mankind, the subtly relentless effects of something akin to *reductio* may become manifest in alarm, fear and even civil unrest. Lest we forget, in the 1940s a certain Mr Goebbels mastered the technique in his propaganda to devastating effect.

We need not allude to such egregious conduct to find examples in our daily lives; maybe not malevolent, perhaps even unintentional, they are misleading nonetheless. Nowhere is this more evident than along that dipstick of societal cohesion – crime statistics.

Perhaps we are all partially responsible since there is always a proportion of the demographic that appeals to the stereotype. Walking along the streets of Glasgow I have hitherto felt no more threatened than when strolling the alleys of my home town in rural Wales. Contrast this with someone who may have been accosted in that same town and consequently experiences apprehension when walking through it again. Sympathetic as I may be, I am unqualified to fully empathise unless I am similarly accosted and until such time the statistics are all but meaningless to me. So, let us mitigate ignorance by peering behind some of the numbers.

The crime rate differs between criminal offences and a generalised figure for the overall crime rate is *per se* mendacious. It is more illustrative to consider one element in isolation. For the purpose of this exercise I choose violent crime as recorded by the Police in the UK which, according to a BBC news item of January 2019 – and who amongst us will argue with the veracity of the BBC – increased by 19% in the year ending September 2018. Gosh, that sounds terrible, is nowhere safe? What was that bit earlier about a manifestation in alarm, fear and even civil unrest? Little wonder there are those who resort to security measures at their homes or even the carrying of offensive weapons outside of them in order, as defendants are wont to say in the dock, 'to protect themselves'.

However, poking this alarming statistic with the pointy stick of impartiality – and this is no sideswipe at those who are entrusted with the thankless task of abridging an intricate brief for the ravenous consumption of soundbite news media – I suggest the complexity of the arguments simplified in the claim of 'a rise of 19%' is setting us on a trail of *reductio* that, in the interests of our mental well-being, needs halting in its tracks.

For starters, in extrapolating the stated rise backwards, assuming similar rises in previous years, there must have been a time not so very long ago when violent crime didn't actually exist. Was nineteenth century London really devoid of violent crime? That is the implication and it is clearly arrant twaddle.

It is easy to find the crime statistics unsatisfactory yet each year we are invited to concur with the inescapable inference that everything is getting so much worse by percentages. Though what do those percentages tell us about the nature of the crime and, in turn, the nature of the society of which we are part? In answer I refer to the tale of Sir Arthur Conan Doyle's Charles Augustus Milverton, an arch blackmailer whom our hero Sherlock Holmes finds contemptible. This is curious considering that Holmes is accustomed to dealing with murderers and other high priests and priestesses of criminality. Why is Milverton so offensive? Holmes himself tells us: 'I would ask you how could one compare the ruffian, who in hot blood bludgeons his mate, with this man who methodically and at his leisure tortures the soul and wrings the nerves in order to add to his already swollen money-bags.'

Should a man, in hot blood, bludgeon his mate at home then remorsefully hand himself in to Police, that is a purple sad private tragedy. But if someone walking home is killed by an anonymous assailant for nothing more than a wallet, this does propagate the perception of more frightening streets. Whilst in each case there is someone dead the differences in circumstances are profound.

The degree of temptation is also relevant. My forebears wistfully recounted tales of the Good Old Days when, such was the spirit of the community, doors were left open with no fear that anyone would steal anything. It seems lost on them that they possessed nothing worth stealing. How times change, and who amongst them, had they lived and prospered into the 21st Century, would have been quite so *blasé* about entrusting their computers, mobile phones, televisions and jewellery unto the munificence of that same community? It's a fair bet their doors would be well and truly bolted long before bedtime. With alarms and CCTV to boot. And perhaps a gated entrance, maybe even a roaming dog behind high fencing. Is this based on reality or engendered by the statistics showing how much theft, too, has once again risen by a considerable percentage this year?

Perhaps the truth lies somewhere between the two but there is no denying the insidious effects of the statistics on our patterns of behaviour. Or indeed our reactions to the behaviour of our fellows. A few years ago an advertisement appeared in a national newspaper featuring a glum-looking and bald Ronnie Biggs, he of the Great Train Robbery of 1963, beaming broadly in the adjoining picture as, thanks to some miracle treatment or other, he was suddenly hirsute with flowing locks. All very jolly, though as one who remembers 1963 I wondered if anyone had troubled to ask the family of Jack Mills, the driver who was coshed during the raid that shocked a nation and who died a broken man a few years later, if they too saw the funny side. Is crime now so endemic that we are becoming desensitised to the point it no longer distresses us, or has perception of crime as related by statistics fuelled an autonomous, almost Darwinian, evolution in response to perceived external dynamics that are at best questionable?

The rise in crime may be a reflection on how we are now encouraged to report it, although this is often accompanied by that most dubious of statements: 'many crimes go unreported'. Sometimes even a percentage figure is placed on the number that go unrecorded; answers on a postcard please if anyone can tell me how it is possible to quantify precisely how much we do not know. By any logical criteria the very notion is ludicrous yet we are guided by the statistics to bemoan the shocking rise of crime rather than home in on the inadequacies of the reasoning. The result is that we gradually become ever so slightly more paranoid with every new set of statistics that Chief Constables deign to reveal in their annual reports.

So, here's a prediction for the next year. Every town will have a sign cautioning us that 'thieves operate in this area'. CCTV cameras will be in ever greater demand, despite us already being one of the most surveilled nations on earth. There will be a call for more Police on the streets. Oh, and violent crime will rise again. Probably by about 19%.

Mind how you go.

POSTSCRIPT

'There's widespread concern that video cameras will use facial recognition software to track our every public move. Far less remarked upon – but every bit as alarming – is the exponential expansion of 'smart' video surveillance networks. Private businesses and homes are starting to plug their cameras into police networks and rapid advances in artificial intelligence are investing closed-circuit television, or CCTV, networks with the power for total public surveillance. In the not-so-distant future, police forces, stores and city administrators hope to film your every move – and interpret it using video analytics. The rise of all-seeing smart camera networks is an alarming development that threatens civil rights and liberties throughout the world. Law enforcement agencies have a long history of using surveillance against marginalised communities, and studies show surveillance chills freedom of expression – ill effects that could spread as camera networks grow larger and more sophisticated.'

The rise of smart camera networks and why we should ban them.
Michael Kwet. 27 January 2020. https://theintercept.com/2020/01/27/surveillance-CCTV-smart-camera-networks/

Seven Monster Raving Loony Party policies which are now part of UK law

24-hour licensing laws
The party campaigned for all day opening of pubs in the 1980s, which became law in 1995. In the 1997 elections they campaigned for all-night opening too.
24-hour drinking became legal in 2005.

Lowering the voting age to 18
Lord Sutch stood as a candidate for his National Teenage Party, later to become Monster Raving Loony Party – their key policy was lowering the voting age from 21 to 18.
Votes for 18 year olds were introduced in 1969.

Abolition of dog licences
It used to be mandatory for dog owners to hold a licence, although it was often ignored.
Dog licences were abolished in 1987.

The legalisation of commercial radio
An early policy of the National Teenage Party: until Radio One started in 1967 there was nothing for teenagers on the BBC, so to hear pop music you had to tune into illegal pirate stations.
The first commercial radio licences were issued in 1972.

The pedestrianisation of Carnaby Street
Lord Sutch had heard from friends in Swinging London's Carnaby Street that traders were finding the increasing congestion hard to deal with. He joined the campaign for pedestrianisation.
The Greater London Council pedestrianised the street in 1973.

Passports for pets
The party made a pledge in their 1983 manifesto to issue pets with passports so that they could travel abroad without lengthy stays in quarantine.
Pet passports were introduced in October 2001.

Abolition of the 11 plus exam
Another policy from the National Teenage Party, because it's "the wrong age to take an exam that affects you for the rest of your life".
The 11 plus was abolished nationally in 1976.

Lord Sutch, founder of the Official Monster Raving Loony Party and its leader from 1983 to 1999

FLAT OR ROUND

Well, is the earth flat or is it round? Or do we in fact live on the inside of the globe (if it is a globe) rather than the outside? In the State of Ohio, at least, it looks like your views and your rights to express them – however 'off the wall' they may be – are about to be enshrined in law.

Late into one miserable autumn night recently, still several steps ahead of the sleep that refused to overtake me and with no disturbance to my long-tolerant other half by my side, I switched on the radio, inserted my earpiece and sought mental emollience via the soothingly erudite vibes of the BBC World Service. I listened languidly as the top-of-the-hour news bulletin followed the Greenwich pips before being shaken from my reverie by a remarkable piece of reportage from the good ol' US of A – where else – declaring The Ohio State House of Representatives has passed legislation that exams mustn't be marked down for non-scientific views provided the reasoning is within principles of expressed religion. What?

It's true; I looked it up on the BBC website later at a more sensible hour. Ohio House Bill 164, known as the Ohio Students Religious Liberties Act includes reasonable clauses such as preventing schools from denying students access to facilities because of their religion. However, controversy has focused on a section that reads: 'Assignment grades and scores shall be calculated using ordinary academic standards of substance and relevance, including any legitimate pedagogical concerns, and shall not penalize or reward a student based on the religious content of their work.' In other words, as was later explained helpfully by local TV station WKRC, provided students offer a 'reasoned argument' they will not be castigated for suggesting that the earth is only 6000 years old. Or, indeed, flat.

Arguably if the bill passes the Senate and is signed by the governor, all students will need to do is find a religion that endorses every error and claim it is their own, and, at least until the law is tested in court, some teachers may be reluctant to criticise unscientific answers in the face of a potential lawsuit arguing they have breached the student's religious liberty. The Ohio Senate has an even more overwhelming Republican majority than the House so at the time of composing this its chances of passage are high.

Whilst I confess to being taken aback by the prospect of a flat earth becoming enshrined in law the premise was not new to me and, falling on my background as an inland waterways devotee, I harkened to the time around twenty years ago when I undertook a modest study for a magazine article in which my opening gambit contained the lines: 'The waterways are not immune to the attentions of those who march to the beat of a different drum and have attracted their share of fruit loops and basket cases over the years, none more so than loyalists of the flat earth theory.'

In light of these developments that now prevent discouragement of – one could even say actively promote – such beliefs, two decades after my original piece I may be obliged by default to revisit my taxonomy of 'fruit loops and basket cases'. So, let's take another look …

One might have thought that the evidence of satellite photographs would have destroyed any vestige of resistance from the flat earth fraternity. Not so. Such evidence is considered a monumental conspiracy as propounded by the likes of the 1950's film *Destination Moon* or latterly *Capricorn One*, both of which reflect scepticism towards the veracity of space exploration. *Capricorn One*, which tells the tale of a government hoax created to deceive the public on a supposed Mars landing, first appeared on screen in 1978 as a barely imaginable futuristic plot. Gosh, the mind boggles what theories will bubble to the top as contemporary plans to actually put humans on Mars approach reality.

Meanwhile, back on our flat earth, the argument is as old as recorded history itself and was equated directly with the literal word of the Bible. In the sixth century the Greek monk Cosmas wrote his *Christian Topography* in which he refuted the 'false and heathen' notion that the earth is a sphere. There's just a couple of religious connections as enshrined in Ohio House Bill 164. History has also been enlivened with pronouncements from such luminaries as Copernicus, Galileo and Newton but it was the Victorians who procured some of the most contentious evidence in support of both camps and they chose as their battleground a section of the Old Bedford Level which lies just on the edge of the Middle Level Navigations. There, that now explains my interest in this quest. The reason for their choice lay in the landscape, a tale which itself goes back thousands of years.

Following the end of the last ice age rising sea levels severed Britain from mainland Europe and flooded the area now known as the Fens. The land became separated from the sea by sand banks and the protection this afforded encouraged dense vegetation that was laid down as peat deposits. By the Norman Conquest these had risen in places above the level of the sea and already housed several settlements.

Flood banks were built from Roman times and although there is further evidence of reclamation works in the Middle Ages it was the seventeenth century before any comprehensive drainage scheme was attempted. Between 1630 and 1655 the Dutchman Sir Cornelius Vermuyden reclaimed much land by massive workings that included the cuts of the Old and New Bedford rivers to bypass the meandering Great Ouse, with storage areas and drainage channels to provide more direct routes to the outfalls.

It was these routes that were eventually to be put to use in a manner that Vermuyden could never have envisaged.

During the golden age of Victorian enlightenment many a noteworthy loon diverted their attentions to an uninterrupted length of about six miles between Welney and Old

Bedford bridges. A nineteenth century realignment of a section to the southwest of Welney eventually compromised further experimentation but I refuse to let this detract from such a ripping yarn of glorious eccentricity in its purest form.

For several months during 1838 Dr Samuel Birley Rowbotham lodged in a hut on the canal bank and conducted a series of experiments, always with the same result. Standing in the canal with his telescope at water level at one bridge he found that, contrary to round-earth theory, which dictated that vessels would disappear from view over the horizon, he could invariably obtain a clear view of canal traffic at the other bridge.

After many more years of research and verification, using his pseudonym Parallax he published *Zetetic Astronomy; Earth Not A Globe* (from the Greek *zeteo*, meaning to seek) which has since been the standard reference for anti-roundearthers.

The work unleashed a glut of opponents who descended on the Old Bedford line and the matter reached fever pitch in 1870 when sizable wagers were placed on the outcome of rival experiments. Independent referees were appointed but when the opposing factions could not even agree on the interpretation of results the matter degenerated into farce.

The findings were placed before a court but following an admirably non-committal adjudication by the Queen's Bench in 1876 the challenge was abandoned unresolved amidst much acrimony on all sides. The controversy raged unabated and the Old Bedford Level continued to be frequented by enthusiasts of both persuasions. In 1905 the irrepressible Lady Blount, a lady to whom I have referred elsewhere in my musings as frequenting the higher echelons of refined idiosyncrasy, led her entourage here with a view to settling the dispute once and for all.

Sometimes known as Zeteo, Lady Elizabeth Anne Mould Blount was a vocal advocate of Flat Earth theory in the late nineteenth and early twentith centuries and one of the creators of the Universal Zetetic Society, the precursor to the Flat Earth Society, founded after Rowbotham's death. Lady Blount was a devout Christian and her writings utilised a mix of scriptural and experimental arguments to support her views.

By means of a technique essentially similar to earlier experiments, in which a white sheet was hung just above the water's edge at one bridge and viewed from the other, her efforts were rewarded with a signed declaration from an independent witness which supported her proposal that the six miles of water, and therefore by inference the earth, were entirely flat.

Lady Blount savoured the afteret alglow of celebrity for some until fading into obscurity but not before asserting via scientific publications and learned journals that the earth's flatness had been scientifically proven.

The Old Bedford Level is not the only waterway to have achieved infamy at the hands of oddballs. In the 1890s Cyrus Teed, self-styled leader of the Koreshan faith of America, confounded both planists and spherists when he proclaimed that the earth is in fact a hollow globe inhabited on its inside surface. The sun, moon, stars and planets are, he postulated, all only a short distance above the outer surface. The horizon therefore, according to Teed, slopes upwards away from the observer, not downwards as in round earth theory or *ad infinitum* as per flat earth theory.

Teed supported this remarkable assertion by means of observations along the Old Illinois Drainage Canal using a device he called a rectilineator, parts of which still survive.

Worldwide the flat earth theory is largely restricted to a few hidden tribes or third-world countries where the concept arises largely through ignorance rather than reasoned thought. However there are pockets of genuine resistance and well considered assertions, or just plain wacky theories depending on your perspective, to the idea of a round earth, notably but not exclusively in southwest Britain and America.

In 1956 Samuel Shenton founded the International Flat Earth Society. Following his death in 1971, Charles K Johnson created the International Flat Earth Society of America and raised membership to 3000. By 1980 this fell to 200. Johnson died in 2001, and the society no longer took in new members until it was revived online in 2004 and officially restarted in 2009.

I confess to being at a loss in offering a coherent explanation as to its resurgence but there is evidence to suggest that the combination of a move towards religious fundamentalism, aided by the explosion in communications technology and social media, may be helping to rekindle planism. Just check the internet, it's full of the stuff. Koreshanity and the inverse globe theory have – for now at least, but who knows? – all but disappeared.

For me, as an *aficionado*, I simply find it fascinating to note the role played by ostensibly unpretentious inland waterways in the propounding of theories fundamental to our interpretations of the universe itself.

So, what's your position; flat or round? Or even Koreshan. Either way, no longer will you be written off as a crank, particularly if you live in Ohio where your views may even enjoy legal protection. And, provided your reasoning is sound, you'll pass all of your exams. Me? Well, I'll just keep steering my boat along the cut in the hope that I don't one day just fall off the end somewhere. Steady as she goes, skipper.

POSTSCRIPT

'Despite Aristotle coming up with the proof the earth is a globe more than 2,000 years ago there are still many people who doubt it. Even images taken of the earth from space can't shake their belief that the planet we call home is a disc, rather than a ball. And flat-earthers are making their controversial views known far and wide. Mark Sargent, who firmly believes the earth is a flat disc, appeared on *This Morning (British daytime television programme – Ed)* and clashed with host Phillip Schofield. Mark insisted there was weather balloon footage of the earth, taken from 120,000 feet, that showed the earth was 'table top flat'. Our Phil was not to be deterred and insisted he had seen the curve of the earth when he flew at 65,000 feet on Concorde. Sargent, like many flat-earth believers, claims the earth is surrounded by a huge wall of ice, which is why we don't fall off. He also claims there is land mass outside this huge wall, which Schofield joked we should all go on holiday to.'

Daily Mirror Online, first appeared 2 May 2018; discovered by the author some eight months after the original podcast was recorded.

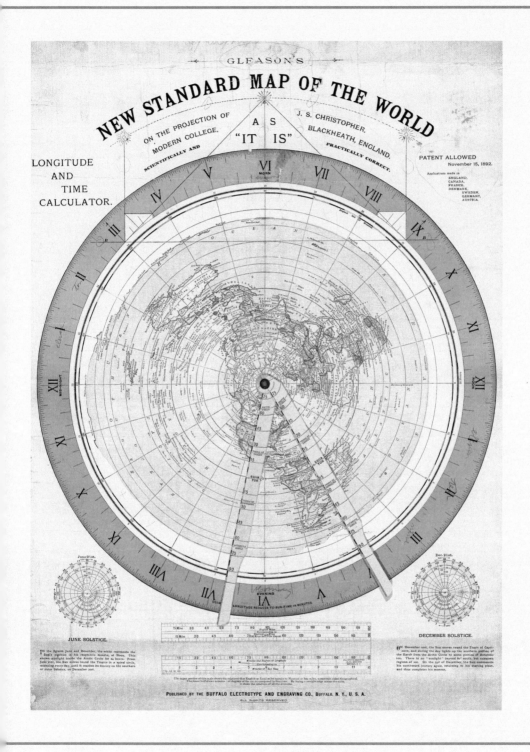

PLURALs DON'T HAVE APOSTROPHES!

Here is a car:
Here are two cars:

It's NOT two car's.

PEAS AND QUEUES

*Our language is constantly evolving yet although
this is inevitable are there some changes that, in the
interests of accurate communication, we should resist?
The apostrophe is dead; long live the apostrophe.
But does it matter, and should we care?*

Shortly after UK decimalisation, which to some of us seems like only yesterday but was in reality 1971, and when those who lived through it were recalibrating ourselves with the new whilst still mourning the comforting familiarities of the old, I was tempted by a colleague to make my inaugural visit into a betting shop.

Here, under his avuncular guidance, I laid a stake for the equivalent of the old 2s/6d, or 12.5 new pence. Imagine my unalloyed joy when some three-legged nag I picked with a pin crossed the line first and I was rewarded with the life-changing sum of 10s/6p, by then better known as 52.5 new pence. Lo, here endeth my first – and only – experience in a 'bookies' since, over half a lifetime down the line, I can still take smug satisfaction in being one of the few people who have made a killing, taken their winnings and left, never to return. From which it may reasonably be inferred that I am not a gambling man.

Even so, I am prepared to lay a sizeable wager that a diminutive snippet of news, tucked in an inside pocket of one continent bursting into flames whilst another drowns under a biblical deluge, will someday be seen as a totemic point of reference in the trajectory of our language.

In early December 2019 it was announced that a society dedicated to preserving the, quote, 'much-abused' apostrophe was to be disbanded. John Richards, who worked in journalism for much of his career, started the Apostrophe Protection Society in 2001 after he retired. Calling it a day he wrote on its website: 'Fewer organisations and individuals are now caring about the correct use of the apostrophe in the English language. We, and our many supporters worldwide, have done our best but the ignorance and laziness present in modern times have won'.

Lest we think this is all too inconsequential for words, if you'll excuse the makeshift allusion, it was a blockbusting little tome of 2003 by literary editor and broadcaster Lynn Truss that exposed the importance of apostrophes, commas, colons, semi-colons and other punctuation marks to an audience that, judging by the sales, was ravenous for redemption.

The title of the book *Eats, Shoots & Leaves: The Zero Tolerance Approach to Punctuation* is a syntactic ambiguity – that is, a verbal fallacy arising from an ambiguous or erroneous grammatical construction – and is derived from a joke about bad

punctuation as explained on the back cover thus, slightly paraphrased:

A panda walks into a café. He orders a sandwich, eats it, then draws a gun and fires two shots in the air. As the panda makes towards the exit he drops a badly punctuated wildlife manual.

The waiter turns to the relevant entry to find an explanation for this strange behaviour. 'Panda. Large black and white bear-like mammal, native to China. Eats, shoots and leaves.' Groan.

To be brutally honest the book itself needed the services of a ruthless Editor and I feel the point was adequately made long before I was a quarter of the way through it, but, hey, it sold in numbers I could never dream of for my modest scribblings so I'll do the noble thing by not tainting the basket with the taste of sour grapes. Anyway, the point is, the proper use of language should start in schools and be continued by parenting but will endure through life by the reading of well-written books – in whatever format of electronic or hard copy they nowadays take.

And therein lies the problem; only the scrupulous Editor, fastidious proof-reader or judicious reviewer, whom by definition must – unlike the casual reader – go through the work with a fine-tooth comb, only they know just how badly many books are written.

Ah, now, I can see the Bard's slings and arrows of outrageous fortune being turned in my direction to repel incursions of intellectual snobbishness but please, hang fire and don't shoot the messenger just yet.

Our wonderful language is constantly morphing; witness the number of words annually included in – and dropped from – that bastion of grammar and usage, the Oxford English Dictionary. Old words become outmoded or unfashionable whilst new ones, particularly those associated with rapid changes in technology, run the gamut on their way from slang or vernacular to mainstream, along with the punctuation that helps steer their interpretation. Many survive the course over the long term and it is said that someone familiar with the Black Country dialect is well equipped to tackle Chaucer, author of *The Canterbury Tales*, who is considered as critical in legitimising the use of Middle English.

As I compose this right now I have in front of me a small library of books defining long-abandoned words and grammar. Truth is, I relish their use and am fascinated by their roots and derivations. I am also besotted by anachronisms that are long out of favour and sadly relegated to the lesser-thumbed recesses of the OED. I adore the oral sensation of rolling my tongue around the likes of *diligrout*, a nobleman's porridge, *gorgayse*, a medieval term for fashionable, or the sixteenth century *pilgarlick*, infinitely more colourful than its mundane analogue of bald-headed.

Occasionally I bring one or two of these relics out of retirement to re-employ for my own pleasure. This is not for pretension but more an act of rebellion against their devaluation. Of course, I recognise that our language is constantly evolving and I do not stand King Cnut-like resisting its march. It's more the case of finding a certain reassurance in the robustness of the time-served yet equally I am amongst the first to acknowledge, nay welcome, how our language transmutes with time and circumstances.

And, taking a lump hammer to further crack the veneer of affectation, patois, dialect and poetic license all play their part. Lewis Carroll's masterpiece of nonsense Jabberwocky in his 1871 novel *Through the Looking-Glass, and What Alice Found There* is an object lesson in how to mangle our native tongue. In 2016 *Solar Bones* by Mike McCormack, an entire book written as a single sentence, won the Goldsmith Prize for fiction that 'breaks the mould or opens up new possibilities in the novel form'. Even the aforementioned Bard himself used the technique of emphasis created by grammatical anomalies, as in 'parting is such sweet sorrow'. Sorrow, sweet ... really?

All notable, though all grammatically incorrect in the usually accepted sense. Which is what, exactly? Well, let's begin to answer that one by asserting that a prerequisite for any language is a structure in which the message is directed from a transmitter to a receiver and downloaded to convey the same meaning as was formulated by the transmitter. To achieve this without a mutually understood structure is all but impossible. It's as if we are communicating in different languages, or different variations of the same language. Which, in fact, we are.

Signs depicting Earl's Court / Earls Court with and without an apostrophe

Riding the hinterland between nebulous thought and accurate expression is unforgiving territory. The structure may not be immediately apparent but it is nonetheless there; I recall the late self-styled 'Professor' Stanley Unwin whose comedic gobbledygook 'Unwinese' was impenetrable but became more coherent when he explained his rules for concocting it. *Et voilà*, he had a structure for his zany language that transgressed negligence of its own parameters.

And therein lies the crux; in exactly the same way that Tommy Cooper could mess up his magic tricks to hilarious effect only because he knew how to do them properly in the first place – he was a leading light in the Magic Circle – I contend that it is possible to adeptly divert the rules of grammar only when one knows how to navigate them properly.

Similarly, compare and contrast the distinction between the increasingly common dropping of apostrophes at, say, Kings Cross or the Regents Canal with blatant misuse when they are thrown in arbitrarily or left out erroneously. *Quod erat demonstrandum* we establish *prima facie* evidence of the distinction between fashionable laziness and unpardonable illiteracy.

I confess this vexes me yet I live with it daily in my perplexity of fathoming my home being Drovers Barn, spelt with no apostrophe. A charming idiosyncrasy that has its own sense of license and at no great loss to its meaning, I ponder whether it was named by a predecessor with a sense of grammatic experimentalism or the possessor of a lamentable measure of ignorance. In either case it is wrong. Then I realise that few who visit here even notice, let alone feel challenged by the inadvertence, and, *ergo*, I understand the dissolution of the Apostrophe Society.

And I fear it is my sad duty to suggest it is not just the poor apostrophe; the battle is far from over as our grammatical *regimen* is indiscriminately mauled by the advent of … take a guess … yes, social media. Demanding little attention span and requiring even less consideration to detail, it is a prime mover in the trend to SHOUT in capitals representing repetitive volume rather than convince by considered persuasion.

Behind every good writer lies an even better Editor yet modern social media enables one to become their own moderator when neither qualified nor competent to do so. Inane abbreviations and puerile emoticons compound downward pressure and the patina of trust from messages sent or retweeted from those we already know gives strength to the perpetuation and acceptance of errors. Amongst these, the rubrics of good syntax and accurate punctuation are just plain inconvenient.

So then, having agitated my little grammatical hornet's nest, and having accepted that language will change, does it matter? And why trouble to constrain it within a universally accepted structure?

In September 1999, after almost ten months travelling to Mars, and when NASA scientists were on tenterhooks with anticipated discoveries on the Red Planet, the eponymous – and hugely expensive – Mars Climate Orbiter plunged into the atmosphere and was destroyed. The reason? Someone had programmed the thrusters using the wrong units of measurement. A cartoon of the time showed a smashed space ship on the Martian surface with the sardonic caption: 'Metric, English, whatever'.

It might just as pertinently have said: 'Eats, shoots and leaves. Please review before take-off.' But why quibble when we can instead bask in the judgement of luminaries such as John C Wells, Professor Emeritus of phonetics at University College London and former President of the English Spelling Society – honestly, you just couldn't make this stuff up – who, in a proclamation that must have been a dagger in the heart of John Richards albeit being berated by then Prime Minister David Cameron, described the apostrophe as 'a waste of time'.

Ah well, for those amongst us less enlightened who obdurately rail behind our anachronistic convictions, there will always be the humourist's firewall of disparaging invective. And, as they say in these parts, *there's* lovely. Now *that's* satire.

POSTSCRIPT

I referred here to 'that bastion of grammar and usage, the Oxford English Dictionary' and the impact of the Coronavius pandemic that engulfed us just a few weeks after this was recorded was indeed subsequently reflected in their website, which said …
'The Oxford Languages 2020 Word of the Year campaign looks a little different to (*sic – see below)* previous years. The English language, like all of us, has had to adapt rapidly and repeatedly this year. Given the phenomenal breadth of language change and development during 2020, Oxford Languages concluded that this is a year which cannot be neatly accommodated in one single word, and we have decided to report more expansively on this in our Words of an Unprecedented Year report'.

The more usual 'Word of the Year' became instead a whole raft of words and expressions that had sprung up in sufficient general usage as to be considered mainstream. No doubt aided in their diffusion by social media at much the same rate as the Covid virus, many of them were associated with that same virus. When the dust settles it may prove that a combination of social media and pandemic has resulted in the most seismic singular shift in our parlance – and, in view of its dissemination, the mode of punctuation – ever recorded.

* Incidentally, and *apropos* nothing in particular, as a youngster at school I was taught that the correct expression was to differ *from* (Latin *di* = apart, *ferro* = carry) hence one could not 'carry apart' *to*, it had to be *from*. The current paradigm suggests that 'different to', 'different from' and now the baffling 'different than' are all acceptable depending on context and whether one is using UK English or American English. In reminding myself of the quip that we are two nations separated by a common language I do not propose pursuing this with the OED (UK) or Webster's (USA). But at least they used the apostrophe.

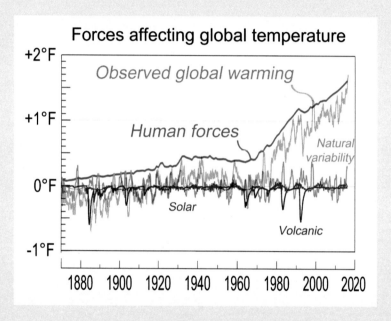

HEAT AND LIGHT

Our insatiable thirst for energy is countered by increasing levels of atmospheric greenhouse gases and the imperative to tackle global warming. But do the established laws of science indicate that, ultimately, our fate may not lie entirely in our hands?

Just about anyone who knows me also knows of my passion for inland waterways. So, no surprise that in making new acquaintances I am invariably asked how far my interest goes back. Hmmm, that's a tricky one, since my mother tells me she always suspected I was born with canal water in my veins rather than blood, but I do distinctly recall a very early schooldays age when both my late father and I yearned to own an ex-army pontoon on which we could strap an outboard engine and innocently pootle down the cut. It's charming naivety is rather laughable to imagine now, especially in view of all the regulations that would have since been brought to bear upon our ventures, but the fact we, or rather he, could only dream of meeting the price tag of twenty quid says much about our circumstances at the time.

Instead he suggested I start a savings policy so that in ten years hence – somewhere towards the end of my life as I saw it at that age – I could buy a boat. Which eventually I did. No fool, my dad. He imbued in me a savings habit that endured to this day and although I neither live in a mansion nor own a tropical island he was instrumental in helping me appreciate the value of fiscal prudence.

But, back to making new acquaintances, the second question is invariably 'well, other than to fish, float a boat or walk down the towpath, what else is there to do?' My stock answer is: 'quite a lot, actually' and after more than half a century of doing exactly that I am better informed to address the query with not a single angler, boater or walker in sight.

My appreciation of our unique inland waterways heritage has always been up there but was focussed as if by a giant magnifying glass during my term of office as an appointee of what was then, in 2012, the new Canal & River Trust, the 'third sector' body that succeeded the old British Waterways.

Here, under the remarkable stewardship of a man who has since become a valued friend, I was afforded free rein to examine any elements I wished to in promoting inland waterways into the 21st Century. Bearing in mind that until not so long ago many of them were at risk of being abandoned or lost forever, the opportunity for me to liberally extol them was music to my ears and I grabbed the score sheet with relish, eager to add my own few notes. In turn I examined the use of technology, in particular the

Recorded 13 February 2020

development of waterways apps and the internet, the promotion of art, the engagement with local communities and, a personal favourite, hydroelectric power generation.

My advocacy of this somewhat arcane aspect stemmed from an earlier involvement with a fledgling hydro-power company that examined the feasibility of installing generators along the River Severn. Not the Severn Barrage which is a totally different concept; we were looking way further inland. Our aspirations were stymied by none other than British Waterways, later the Canal & River Trust, who as preferred bidders were already some way ahead of us so we accepted the inevitable and withdrew. However, I am delighted that in the interim several hydro operations have appeared on our inland waterways and, during my stint with CRT I was able to offer a contribution to their development from an independent perspective.

The point of explaining all this is that whilst I was doing so, it helped coalesce vague misgivings I had harboured since my student days into what was to become a palpable concern.

That there is a need for alternatives to fossil-fuelled energy is doubted only by climate change deniers. President Donald Trump will be remembered for his relentless drive for unfettered fossil energy development. He is, of course, not alone and whilst I am being entreated to play my part by buying a re-usable coffee cup and ditching my plastic drinking straw the Chinese are reportedly financing hundreds of coal-fired power stations both at home and in other countries. Australia is not much less tarnished in its use of coal for generation, nor is India. There are many others vying for a place on the carbon footprint roll-of-shame and it makes for uncomfortable reading but let me avoid digressing into politics by instead nailing my colours to the mast in expressing how my personal loyalties lie with hydroelectricity.

Such penchant is shared by my Celtic other half, who was alongside me in the power company venture, since the Scottish government, who have invested massively in the stuff, evidently think likewise. Although in truth they have also invested in other forms of renewables, notably wind generation, that I suspect is part of a coordinated plan to be self-sufficient come what they see as inevitable independence. From the borderland southern uplands northwards the majestic backdrop is desecrated in every direction by forests of hideous rotating blades but hey, this is progress. Or so we are encouraged to believe. Hydro is up to 90%-plus efficient and whilst much of Scotland's is at 'high head' water levels there are 'low head' generators (i.e. less than a couple of metres) around Europe that are still working quietly and efficiently decades after their installation.

Compare and contrast with the aforementioned wind generation, currently flavour of the month with our government south of the border, that provides clean electricity as long as the wind blows. But just how clean, exactly? The manufacture of the turbines involves massive outlay and depletion of resources for an item that at best works at less than 30% efficiency – my figures, but they're as good as the next man's – and all for a puny lifespan of around thirty years.

Although a relatively new technology there are already companies springing up who ponder what to do with the first generation of the things. Landfill for all but the small proportion of recyclable bits seems the most likely option. Which surely goes some way toward defeating the object.

Solar panels are equally short term and again use finite and increasingly rare resources for a brief lifespan after which they must be disposed of; again, a problem. Don't even get me started on batteries – the electric vehicle may seem a personal transport utopia, but do give a thought to how those batteries are made in the first place, and what happens to them and their toxic legacy when they wear out. Which is not very long. Then there's the nuclear option and various others that fall within the gambit of 'clean' energy but I am drawing a line under all of them and their merits – or otherwise – right now in pursuit of the wider issue that exercises me greatly.

It is an issue fundamental to every single form of energy production and I am frankly astonished that no politician, climate change advocate or even the scientific community has yet publicly addressed it since it is an objective fact that has roots predating Einstein by the thick end of fifty years. It is, quite simply, the three laws of thermodynamics. If that sounds just too complicated, trust me, it's not and although their derivations lie in lots of maths and equations the principles are quite straightforward.

* The first law of thermodynamics, also known as Law of Conservation of Energy, states that energy cannot be destroyed. That's it. Easy peasy. Next …

* The second law of thermodynamics states that the thermal equilibrium of any 'isolated system' always increases. Thus the thermal equilibrium of our solar system, the ultimate 'isolated system', is constantly increasing.

* The third law predicts that the ultimate demise of the ever-expanding solar system; when it has finally expanded all that it can, will be by 'heat death' resulting in a static state of absolute zero temperature.

But that's a few billion years down the line yet, so let's examine what the second law predicts us will happen in the meantime.

The implication of the second law is reinforced by Einstein's theories of special and general relativity and his iconic $E=mc^2$ in which energy and matter are inter-related but can never be destroyed. It is this law that states – and here is the nub of my concern – *it is impossible to continue creating energy from matter without simultaneously producing intractable amounts of waste heat.*

The entire universe, including insignificant little Planet Earth, is inexorably warming and as long as we generate energy by whatever means, hydro, solar, wind, fossil fuels, nuclear, you name it, we can only add to a problem from which there is no subtraction. This puts the whole issue of how we produce the energy into the context that no matter how we produce it, the second law expressly states that our production of the energy will inevitably produce heat.

At risk of sounding heretical I contend that the build-up of CO_2 in the atmosphere is in this context almost a red herring, get rid of all the CO_2 you like; however clean or dirty we may be producing energy the ultimate consequence of producing it is more and more heat. It may be billions of years down the line but the third law predicts what ultimately awaits if mankind is around to witness it, which, given our penchant for messing up the planet in our way with or without the intervention of the laws of thermodynamics, seems unlikely by a long shot.

Wow; that puts a bit of a different complexion on it, does it not? Please do remember these are the laws of science – I am simply articulating them as incompetently as I can. But if my interpretation holds water, little wonder nobody has yet stood at the dispatch box and identified it as such. For minds attuned to political cycles rather than 'billions of years down the line' this may be understandable. But a continuing collective silence could be considered mendacious.

Perhaps I am ranting at a tangent – this is, after all, just *In My Opinion* so others may draw different conclusions, yet I confess to already having sought clarification by submitting my thoughts to various authorities, not least a well known Professor of such things who is now a respected TV and radio personality. I did this some years ago before he was quite so famous so I accept he is maybe now too busy with his media appearances and scientific career to be troubled by my little query. Suffice to say, I have yet to receive a response either from him or anyone else. I wonder why?

Meanwhile, I note those wind turbines are being built simultaneously with dirty fossil fuel and doomsday nuclear power stations, the hydro plants are vying for attention with solar panels and batteries and the thermal springs are pumping alongside so-called natural yet hardly carbon-neutral gas.

And still it gets hotter, and hotter, and hotter. Phew

POSTSCRIPT

The UK's exertions to, quite literally, clean up its act extend across the gamut from support of political initiatives to the phasing out of 'dirty' energy sources. Collectively they are not perfect but they are an encouraging start. They are also a powerful statement of intent from a tiny nation that, in the aspirational stakes at least, punches well above its own weight. The phasing out of all remaining UK coal-fired power stations should be attained by 2024.

Unfortunately there are many nations who are not as yet moved by our laudable example and the continuing use of coal on a grand scale must be of concern to the climate change lobbyists. The statistics are alarming. Or alarmist, depending on how they are interpreted. An interrogation of that contemporary mainstay of reportage, the internet, can further complicate matters by being confusing and, in some instances, frankly mendacious. Headlines such as: 'China Is Still Building an Insane Number of New Coal Plants' (*Wired Magazine* 27 November 2020), 'China continues to increase its coal power, but in India new construction has ground to a near halt' (sub-edit: *The Guardian* 3 August 2020) and 'Japan Races to Build New Coal-Burning Power Plants' (*New York Times* 3 February 2020) point an accusatory finger in the direction of Asia and the Far East and certainly grab the attention in offering up a bogey-man or two.

But before we get too smug, we may reflect on what is happening both in Europe: 'We won't let Germany build a new coal power plant. German activists plan in 2020 to block Datteln 4, the only coal power plant under construction in Western Europe, and push Berlin to exit coal.' (*Climate Home News* 9 January 2020) and in the USA, where the Make America Great Again *mantra* of a Trump presidency has led in some states to a revitalised enthusiasm for coal.

Down under in Australia, itself no stranger to the use of the black rock, the eponymous Australia Institute claims to be 'the country's most influential progressive think tank, conducting research on a broad range of economic, social and environmental issues in order to inform public debate and bring greater accountability to the democratic process'. It recently compiled an analysis, *Deconstructing the case for coal,* based on a report supported by several widely-respected organisations including Greenpeace, entitled *Boom and Bust 2018; tracking the global coal plant pipeline.*

In debunking broad-brush claims such as 'Sixty countries have coal-fired capacity under construction' and 'China is currently building over 600 power stations' – as seen in several sources but likely 'sent viral' by copy and paste – the Institute acknowledges the continuing use of coal but draws distinction between those being built versus those scheduled for closure or already decommissioned, cancelled projects, new-build stations and those undergoing upgrade or equipment replacement. As usual the truth is probably in the mix somewhere and merely needs extracting in the same way one removes broken eggs from an omelette and I invite the reader to make their own enquiries in reaching a ,.. In this context I am personally more exercised by both the degree of tilt on the playing field and the pace of securing an internationally coordinated policy to address a global concern.

However, it would be wholly inaccurate to create any impression of unrelenting negativity so I counterbalance with a few notes of optimism;

For the first time solar power generation has outpaced coal and the use of coal is expected to be phased out worldwide by 2025. Solar and wind power are now cheaper than coal; *The International Renewal Energy Agency* reports that 'Renewables Increasingly Beat Even Cheapest Coal Competitors on Cost' (2 June 2020). And it is now cheaper to build a solar farm than the equivalent coal-powered variant.

'Environment award for man who stopped new coal power plant in Ghana' read the headline: A climate activist has been awarded a prestigious Goldman Environmental Prize for leading a grassroots campaign to stop a new coal-fired power station being built in Ghana. Chibeze Ezekiel worked with local communities to highlight the damage the power station would have caused, and persuaded his government that renewable energy was the way forward. (*BBC Online* 30 November 2020)

It is clear that King Coal, having reigned almost unchallenged for centuries, is imminently about to be deposed and sent into exile.

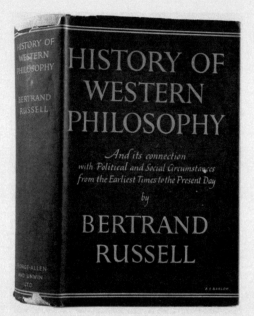

1945 First edition

AGE OF REASON

A long-defunct grammar school, a pupil in the 'shallow waters' of his formative years and a celebration of half a century since the death of one of our greatest intellects, Graham reflects on how this rich combination may have inadvertently led to unintended consequences.

Rowley Regis Grammar School sat atop the Rowley Hills overlooking the Stour Valley with magnificent views across Clent and beyond. On a hot summer's day the heat inversion caused the emissions from Round Oak Steel Powders in Brierley Hill to engulf all in an orange dome set against a backdrop of green rolling hills and powder blue skies dotted with cotton ball clouds. It probably blighted more people with respiratory problems than twenty fags a day but it did look stunning. And the school was itself an impressive looking edifice when viewed from the orange glow upwards. It was brand new, modern and a pinnacle of local educational attainment of its time.

The project started life down in the valley in Wrights Lane, Old Hill, using Victorian premises vacated by the local Central School. It became a Grammar School in 1948. After persistent lobbying by the headmaster Mr George T. Lloyd that the premises were unfit, the new school was built in Hawes Lane, Rowley Regis and opened in September 1962. It remained for a mere thirteen years until Sandwell MBC closed it in July 1975 as part of a phasing-out of grammar schools in favour of comprehensive education. After further alternate use, by 2008 this short-lived seat of learning had been demolished entirely and redeveloped such that little trace of the original remains.

How times, and attitudes, change and it seems that for some the very notion of grammar schools now sticks in the craw like cock-fighting or eating red meat. On reflection, since the concept of Grammars was rooted in churning out a steady stream of administrators to oversee the colonies of an Empire that no longer existed, they may have a point. Even so, as a pupil from 1965 through to the class of 1972 I was fortunate, and rather proud, to undertake all of my secondary education there and to attain my modest clutch of O and A levels, as they were then known, before moving on.

I use the word *fortunate* advisedly; I was fortunate, *not* privileged – very few of my council house counterparts would ever consider ourselves that – and it was but for the support of my decidedly working-class parents that I ever got there, let alone stayed the course.

An expression attributable to several but notably George Bernard Shaw is that youth is wasted on the young. That being so, then *mea culpa*, although in my defence no more so than any other teenager from the past one thousand generations; nothing changes. The challenge is more to recognise, and accept, when youth has receded and there is less life remaining than what has gone before. Armed with such critical reflection one may begin to atone for careless extravagances of the past and perhaps gain valued insight into what this life-thing is all about.

But back to my grammar school and the man who spearheaded the drive for it, the formidable George T. Lloyd whose reputation as an educator was writ large. He was also a Justice of the Peace, which likely manifested itself in his approach to discipline. To the pupils of Rowley Grammar he was known universally as 'The Gaffer' and was held in a combination of dread fear and unquestioned respect. To our parents I suspect his setting the bar high gave comforting affirmation that their charges were in capable hands.

Mr Lloyd was a stickler for early morning assembly, that compulsory period of pious Christian readings, solemn music, prayers, songs and an address by The Man Himself before the school day began in earnest. How many schools still do that? Anyway, it was one such morning address in 1970 that The Man Himself gravely informed us that Bertrand Russell had died. Pause for reverent silence. Back to reality. Bertrand who? I pondered for a while before returning to the metaphorical shallow end where I splashed irreverently with my contemporaries, as one of that age does, without giving second glance toward the deep end where so much more lay waiting but which brings responsibilities for self-determination.

Perhaps that defines the transition from youthful *braggadocio* to mature contemplation, that hurdle between the shallows and the depths. We all handle it in our own way; for me it has been an evolving recognition that the works of the great thinkers may hold the key to another door that I now need to negotiate in my continuing travels along Shakespeare's mortal coil. There's no compulsion to do so, but it is all too easy to become stuck in a comfortable rut.

So I began to familiarise myself – become acquainted, I claim no more intellectual rigour than that – with the thoughts of the great philosophers. I quickly learnt philosophy comprises many sub groups; logic, metaphysics, existentialism, ethics, epistemology, aesthetics, the list goes on. I am also more impressed by those who maintain an unbroken line of reasoning without the need to introduce the concept of a God to bridge difficult conceptual gaps. This should not be taken as indicative of agnosticism, I simply find it unconvincing to develop strands of coherent thought that are then held together by the glue of dubious deities, the existence of which, by definition, cannot be proven. But let me not digress; where does this fit into my tale?

Well, it is a tale of pure coincidence since I was minding my business strolling around my adopted home of Hay-on-Wye recently when I stumbled across a hardback book in one of the town's numerous book shops. *Russell Remembered* is a charming account written in 1970 by fellow philosopher Rupert Crawshay-Williams who came to know Russel well in the final twenty-five years of his life. Remarkably, although by this time Russell was already seventy-five he was still yet to harvest some of his finest crops. Escorted back to my schooldays, the front cover sparked me to remember Russell too, and on impulse I bought it for the princely sum of a couple of quid.

It was that same day, shortly after acquiring the book, I realised that The Gaffer's announcement of Russell's death on 2 February 1970 found me here, exactly fifty years later almost to the day, making my move over that hurdle; my youthful disdain at last confined to where it should henceforth remain; in the past. It was quite cathartic.

Over the next few days I devoured *Russell Remembered* and realised that the early part of my life overlapped with that of a genius, the greatest philosopher this country – possibly the world – has ever produced. What is even more uncanny is that he was born just a short jaunt down the road in Monmouth and spent time with the Clough-Ellis family at Portmeirion, a favourite haunt of mine.

Bertrand Arthur William Russell, 3rd Earl Russell, OM FRS (1872–1970) was a philosopher, logician, mathematician, historian, writer, essayist, social critic, political activist, and Nobel Laureate. In the early twentieth century Russell led the British 'revolt against idealism'. He is one of the founders of analytical philosophy. He is widely held to be one of the twentieth century's premier logicians and co-wrote *Principia Mathematica*, an attempt to create a logical basis for mathematics. Russell was a prominent anti-war activist and went to prison for his pacifism during WWI. In 1950, he was awarded the Nobel Prize In Literature 'in recognition of his varied and significant writings in which he champions humanitarian ideals and freedom of thought'. One of his protégés was a young Ludwig Wittgenstein, the harbourer of a ferocious intellect that anyone except the cognoscenti usually finds impenetrable.

Russell's monumental *A History of Western Philosophy* published in 1945 is an examination of Western Philosophy from the pre-Socratic era to the early twentieth century. It attracted some criticism for lack of depth particularly from the post-Cartesian period, but nevertheless became a *Magnum Opus* that has remained in print ever since. When Russell was awarded the Nobel Prize, *A History of Western Philosophy* was cited as one of the books that won him the award and its success secured an income through the latter part of his life.

His eloquence is as mesmerising as it is incisive. Here are a few examples:

On his views of the existence of God, he clarifies his stance effortlessly: 'I do not pretend to be able to prove that there is no God. I equally cannot prove that Satan is a fiction. The Christian god may exist; so may the gods of Olympus, or of ancient Egypt, or of Babylon. But no one of these hypotheses is more probable than any other: they lie outside the region of even probable knowledge, and therefore there is no reason to consider any of them.' It is not difficult to see why I quickly warmed to this man.

As for definition: 'The point of philosophy is to start with something so simple as to not seem to be worth stating and to end with something so paradoxical that no-one will ever believe it'.

And this, even now, a lesson for our times: 'To teach how to live without certainty, and yet without being paralysed by hesitation, is perhaps the chief thing that philosophy, in our age, can still do for those who study it.'

Learning is a series of events that brings about a relatively permanent change in behaviour. It evidently need not be instantaneous and, fifty years down the line, my early exposure to Russell has bought about, albeit belatedly, a relatively permanent change in behaviour that has realigned my own direction of travel. In other words, I have learnt. For those who are now in their teens and splashing in the shallows with energetic detachment, well, youth is still wasted on the young. Yet they are young just once, so let them enjoy it. And please do let us not be too envious of their good fortune in still being at the distant end of the pool in which we, too, once splashed in abandon.

And that, I would suggest, is a conundrum that ought to be addressed by any education system that seeks to embrace both immediacy and longevity; the balance between what is taught now in preparation for impending adulthood and that which is subliminally retained and which may offer sustenance more than half a lifetime down the line when the physicality may have changed but the soul still requires nourishment.

Ah, well; it is a never-ending cycle that I do not envisage deviating too much in the foreseeable future. Boys and girls will continue to be boys and girls. In the meantime, as age inevitably creeps up on me and it seems every day more bits start to creak, I draw comfort from the words of Winston Churchill: 'We are happier in many ways when we are old than when we were young. The young sow wild oats, the old grow sage'.

POSTSCRIPT

This, from *BBC Online* 30 January 2020 ...

'Previously unheard recordings made by the philosopher Bertrand Russell have been discovered by the BBC ahead of the 50th anniversary of his death.

Russell is regarded as one of the most significant British minds of the twentieth century – an eminent philosopher, an anti-war activist and a social critic. The tapes were recorded at his home in north Wales. They are part of the collection, alongside his suits, smoking pipes, letters and artworks.

In the later years of his life, Bertrand Russell and his American wife Edith acquired a reel-to-reel Tandberg tape recorder. Together they recorded hours of material, much of it containing spontaneous discussions. The tapes offer new insights into his life, humour and behind-the-scenes influences. Russell reads his own short stories, talks with neighbours in north Wales, and recalls his travels in China in 1921.

The collection is kept by the Bertrand Russell Peace Foundation, which was formed in 1963 to continue Russell's work for peace, human rights and social justice. Tony Simpson, the foundation's director, says: 'Whilst moving premises, we discovered vinyl, tape and film recordings of Russell, which are being collated in collaboration with the official Bertrand Russell Archives at McMaster University, Canada. Hearing Russell laugh and converse is a remarkable way to encounter one of the most discerning minds of the twentieth century who, fifty years on, attracts new enthusiasts worldwide.'

The piece is accompanied by a beautifully crafted encomium from Amal Rajan, Media Editor BBC:

'I have a lot of heroes, but Bertrand Russell has a special place among them. He was the figure held up by my father as the Great English Mind in whose footsteps I should follow, and thereby justify the sacrifice he and my mum made in coming to this country when I was three.

I think about this every hour of every day. Alas, various tentative steps that I may have taken in that direction swiftly revealed my enormous shortcomings as a mathematician and logician (Russell's first pursuit as a student), chief among them that I had no aptitude for fractal geometry – and indeed all the other subjects Russell mastered when he read for the Mathematical Tripos at Cambridge.

Nor have I, so far, so much as come within sight of his shadow when it comes to writing clear prose, or pumping out great works of philosophy. I could pretend there's still time, but time isn't really the issue.

There is a funny scene in *How to Break Into the Elite*, a documentary produced by Clare Hix which I presented last year, about three minutes in. My dad reveals that he wants me to win the Nobel Prize (though, much to my chagrin, he never specifies which one). A lot of people found this scene really hilarious. To me, the actual joke was that my dad wasn't joking at all. He is very serious about this ambition – and again, the model is Russell, who won the Nobel Prize for Literature.

I think about that every day too. My dad has a thing for reciting poetry and great prose, which I have imbibed. Growing up, he would reach up to the shelf and pull down volumes of Russell's best work, like *In Praise of Idleness* and *Why I am Not a Christian*, and read aloud.

To my mind, Russell gave us the best prose of anyone writing in English in the twentieth century. I try to emulate his style, which combines moral force, erudition, and plain English with unique wit and humanity. That's why I set up The Russell Prize. Of course, I know I'll never come close to Russell's prose calibre.

Where there is evidence, no one speaks of "faith." We do not speak of faith that two and two are four or that the earth is round. We only speak of faith when we wish to substitute emotion for evidence.

Bertrand Russell

fb.com/WFLAtheism

Imagine my glee then, when Alva White, a brilliant BBC producer, approached me to say that she had uncovered some never before heard voice recordings by the great man. To say I was excited would be an understatement. Thanks to Alva's masterful mixing and production, we got a package of unheard Russell onto the *Today* programme.

And if that doesn't keep my dad happy then frankly I'm stuffed.'

With acknowledgement to *BBC Online*.

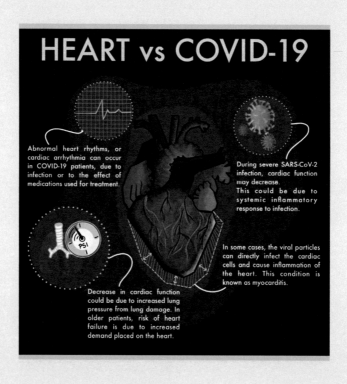

HEART vs COVID-19

Abnormal heart rhythms, or cardiac arrhythmia can occur in COVID-19 patients, due to infection or to the effect of medications used for treatment.

During severe SARS-CoV-2 infection, cardiac function may decrease.
This could be due to systemic inflammatory response to infection.

In some cases, the viral particles can directly infect the cardiac cells and cause inflammation of the heart. This condition is known as myocarditis.

Decrease in cardiac function could be due to increased lung pressure from lung damage. In older patients, risk of heart failure is due to increased demand placed on the heart.

BEHIND THE
BARRICADES

The coronavirus pandemic is of worldwide concern as the race is on to reduce transmission and develop a vaccine. Yet beyond the medical concerns, what implications are there for the eventual resumption of our 'normal' way of life and even upon the state of our democracy?

I find myself in something of a quandary. As I gaze languidly from my office across the Wye valley to the Black Mountains beyond I recognise I am in the company of millions of others who for some days passed have, at our Government's request, been obligingly 'self-isolating' – in other words, staying out of circulation – in, and here's a new term – a 'lockdown'. The ramifications of this mean that other than for occasional jaunts to acquire food from shelves stripped bare as if by locusts, or locusts with a serious bowel problem it would seem from the empty toiletry section, to take exercise (one session a day, mind you) or for medical requirements, we must remain in our hermetic bubbles at no closer than two metres from our fellow humans, who may in any event be unrecognisable behind a face mask and other personal protection paraphernalia.

The reason for all of this, you guessed, is the Coronavirus pandemic of 2020, a newly emerged virus officially tagged Covid-19. Dubbed by the popular media, and with no originality whatsoever, as 'the silent killer' (from heart attacks to carbon monoxide poisoning how many of those are there now?) Covid-19 first subtly pinged the radar in China sometime between late 2019 and early 2020. Within days, and aided greatly in its travels by our modern transport systems, it had embarked on its merciless march round the globe, inflicting severe respiratory symptoms and, for those of great age or with underlying medical conditions, more stark consequences including an unpleasant death.

And therein lies my quandary; the media world is ablaze with reportage. So, on the one hand, recognising there are those far more eminently qualified than I to comment on a debate that is already massively oversubscribed, I am reticent to cloud the waters by chucking in my own two pen'orth. However, as one whose c.v. includes the description 'writer and broadcaster', for the sake of credibility I feel duty-bound to contribute something to what is one of the most significant world events in my lifetime. Compounding my dilemma is the millstone of an otherwise flattering epithet as 'an observer of the unusual and the arcane'. So that settles it. *(Stage directions for film version:* author turns to computer keyboard and with half-sigh of resigned acceptance commences typing.)

I can offer but a snapshot of how affairs stand since a) we are told this pandemic is unprecedented – which, as I will clarify shortly, is hardly accurate – and b) because it is a new variant any forecast is riddled with uncertainty. Thus best to consider this as an entry in my diary on an unspecified day, though the latest news that our Prime Minster is imminently despatching a letter to every house in the land may help nail it close to the nearest one.

Largely as a consequence of those who imagined they know better or who grab the opportunity as some perverse justification for defiance, the Government request to self-isolate has, after just a few hours, been reinforced by the more compulsive introduction of Police powers of enforcement; powers that we are assured, *natch*, will only be exercised under extreme circumstances.

This is good ol' Blighty after all, and other than for the occasional aforementioned transgressors, our traditional British stiff upper lip has anecdotally rendered us more acquiescent to authority than Johnny Foreigner. Yet these are early days and there is the prospect of many more *diktats* to come before the sirens sound the all-clear.

The consequence of this is that our tiny hamlet, the decibels measurement of which rarely enters double figures, is even more pointedly quiet, with passers-by reduced to a level that statisticians would describe as effectively zero. Bliss; at least this aspect of our quarantine is not burdensome.

Living with a mother who by dint of her age requires an extra degree of caution, and with my other half and I no longer being in the first flush of youth, we are sufficiently stocked (not stock*piled*, I hasten to add) with fuel and essentials to the point we needn't worry too much just yet about venturing past the gate. And so, in true Bulldog spirit, we are making the most of our lot by looking for a bright side.

Our incarceration offers more quality time together. We all get along very well, but tensions in the closest of families may fester under such conditions so the fact that they have yet to do so means, even in these difficult times, I have grounds to consider myself fortunate. In the longer-term cabin fever may set in so we are already planning a programme of tasks and activities to mitigate the likelihood.

In years to come this will doubtless be regarded as a period in history, an interesting area of social research. Right now, for those living through it, this nasty little virus is holding the entire world in a grip of uncertainty as frantic attempts are made to reduce transmission, stymie its effects and find a vaccine. To suggest it could lead to an overwhelming of our domestic systems is no exaggeration; it has elsewhere. It knows no barriers and is indiscriminate in its attack, from commoners to Royalty even our Prime Minster and members of his Government, although there is an undeniable irony in suggestions that the latter may have contracted the virus by breaching their own isolation rules.

It will take some time for us to return to how life was like pre-Covid-19, if indeed we ever do. One thing is for sure; I predict with confidence a spike in the world of esoterics.

Artists are notoriously creative in adversity; it is what helps define our humanity.

Worrying as all this may be the situation is not unique and, as I implied earlier, history is strewn with epidemics and pandemics right back to the dawn of civilisation. In 430BC the city of Athens experienced a typhoid-like epidemic that lasted for five years. Moscow was ravaged in the 1770s as was Marseilles around the same time. America has suffered several crippling epidemics since the days of the Founding Fathers; in the 21st Century Africa has been blighted by Ebola.

On the grander scale of *pan*demics the Black Death of the fourteenth century decimated around half the population in its wake from Asia to Europe. The Spanish Flu of 1918 killed an estimated 50 million people from the South Seas to the North Pole whilst in the 1950s Asian Flu claimed over a million lives. More recently we have seen, amongst others, H1N1 swine flu and, of course, HIV/Aids.

Understandably there are those who point to the death toll from Covid-19 being, for now, far less than what is sustained during our seasonal flu epidemics. But such simplicity is to miss the point; existing illnesses follow patterns that have subsequently been analysed and are thus, to a degree, predictable in what scientists call its 'curve of progress'. This novel Covid-19 has not yet fully yielded its parameters. Furthermore, unlike the days of pandemics from a hundred years ago, our systems of communications and transportation are an Achilles heel. Whilst our medicines and vaccines are at levels incomparable with the past, the ability for infection to be inadvertently transported far and wide very quickly means that we may be thrown on to the back foot before a treatment gets its boots on.

So, bearing in mind this is a snapshot of how matters seem to me right now, what is the global reaction? Well, surprisingly in view of us all facing a common threat that one would reasonably imagine justifies a coordinated response, and notwithstanding our unprecedented ability to communicate instantly, the messages are mixed. Each continent or major block is exercising its own interpretations; even members of the European Union, never a group known for its rapid decision-making, are reportedly being distracted by internecine disagreements. Whilst regrettable it is understandable if one delves into the roots of its players.

A nation's values and *mores* are inevitably based on a core philosophy that has been extant, and specific to that nation since earliest times. No one group should claim intellectual or moral superiority over another and we are better advised to understand the differences if we are to constructively engage rather than create conflict by exacting one upon another in some futile gesture of eminence. The West's attempts to impose democracy upon lands that historically have entertained no concept of the democracy we are seeking to impose is ample testament to that.

The American 'right to bear arms' is sacrosanct, albeit its original interpretation as being 'in security of a free State' has since been mangled almost beyond recognition, lies at the heart of that nation's concept of freedom. Thus does President Trump fly full in the face of scientific advice in suggesting Americans will soon be *free* – note the word – to resume their normal lives within a hopelessly optimistic timescale that is recognised by no-one else in possession of an IQ numerically larger than their shoe size.

Compare and contrast with China and the far east, where the teachings of, notably, Confucius, manifest themselves in a model of serenity and order. Then consider how that 'order' is routinely reinforced by suppression of the facts. In Indo–Aryan culture the ancient epic Sanskrit texts of Ramayana and Mahabharata underpin the liturgy of Hinduism, Buddhism, and Jainism. The innate *Karma* is the sum of a person's actions and previous states of existence that decides their fate in future existences.

In the light of these disparities it is hardly surprising that nations may find issue in identifying a common datum. Mercifully, unlike in the past, we have expansive means to maximise the potential to draw together as closely as our dissimilarities permit.

We will pull through this pandemic, of that I am sure, and I do not wish to appear glib in suggesting society has done so before and will one day have to do so again. My greatest apprehension here is the loss of life incurred by the time that we do.

Another concern is the pernicious effects of 'lockdown', a distasteful term that although broadly tolerable in the circumstances is already attracting the attentions of the civil rights movement. The UK is one of the most surveilled nations on earth yet who will be the first to suggest that 'for our greater safety' certain elements of lockdown should be retained after the contagion is arrested. Those who hold power are disinclined to relinquish it. Lest this seems implausible, consider the parlous state of Turkish liberties since their widespread suppression following the 2016 attempted *coup d'état*. Will *we* ever fully trust *our* Government and leaders again, and how will this ultimately impinge upon our democracy?

In his 2018 interview with the BBC's Evan Davis, Sir David Attenborough again spoke of our unsustainable population growth and the urgent need to address it. 'All of our environmental problems become easier to solve with fewer people' he said. Fair point. But not like this, Sir David; surely not like this.

POSTSCRIPT

'As we focus on the day-to-day stresses of our lives our fears for our family, our own health, jobs or business it can be pretty hard to take a step back and realise just what a momentous era we are experiencing, one that historians will be studying for years to come'. (Preamble to interview with SNP's Nicola Sturgeon by Martha Kearney, BBC Radio 4 *Today* 30 November 2020)

At the time of writing the proposed roll out of not one but three different vaccines, all developed in record time since the outbreak of Covid-19, offers some hope that the worst of this nightmare may soon be confined to that 'period in history' alluded to in the main text. A fourth, Russia's 'Sputnik V' is being administered whilst still undergoing mass testing. This has raised some eyebrows but developers claim 'it is 95% effective and causes no major side effects'. More vaccines are already in the pipeline.

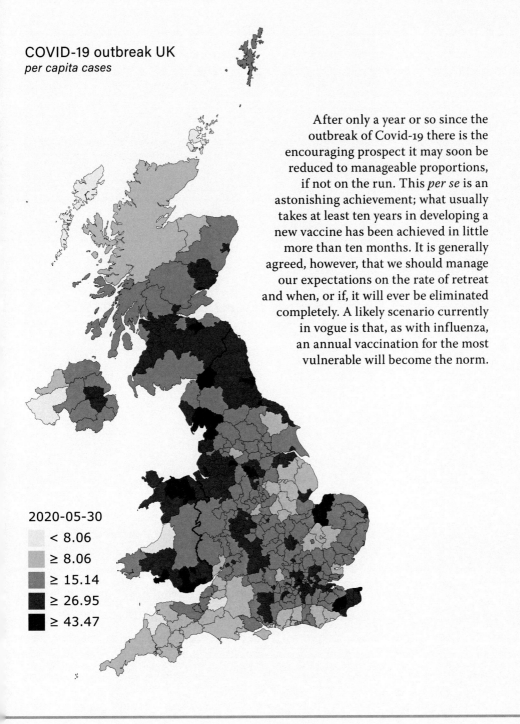

COVID-19 outbreak UK
per capita cases

After only a year or so since the outbreak of Covid-19 there is the encouraging prospect it may soon be reduced to manageable proportions, if not on the run. This *per se* is an astonishing achievement; what usually takes at least ten years in developing a new vaccine has been achieved in little more than ten months. It is generally agreed, however, that we should manage our expectations on the rate of retreat and when, or if, it will ever be eliminated completely. A likely scenario currently in vogue is that, as with influenza, an annual vaccination for the most vulnerable will become the norm.

2020-05-30

< 8.06
≥ 8.06
≥ 15.14
≥ 26.95
≥ 43.47

Ludwig Wittgenstein

THOUGHTS ON THOUGHTS

As civil unrest and protests sweep across a world still reeling from the coronavirus pandemic, inequality and suppression are feeding a mood for change. GF ponders whether philosophy may offer a path towards a more level playing field on which that change may be grounded.

Whilst outward appearances may be superficially masked by a fashionable social patina of the day, the underlying health of a society can be gauged by the collective state of its institutions and social *mores* with an accuracy that Sherlock Holmes might have affirmed as 'not conclusive but certainly suggestive.'

Consider, for example, the burgeoning of weight-watching associations in the UK, the USA and elsewhere in what we refer to as 'the western world'. Nothing wrong with that, who am I to say I couldn't do with losing a few pounds myself? But compare and contrast with the numerous 'third world' countries that, through diverse causes from drought to locusts, are perpetually on the brink of famine and one is hard pushed to find any commensurate growth in slimming clubs. Or nail bars; and dare I include those catering for the vanities in alternatively tanning and bleaching intimate parts of the anatomy; *etcetera, etcetera, etcetera* – well, I rest my case.

And that case is, to express it crudely, the extent to which we are exercised by or actively in pursuit of matters that, to others, might be considered shallow, even inane, is conversely a reflection on the inherent strength of our society, No great risk of famine, no immediate threat of war, no sign of pestilence on the horizon (until recently, that is); we can afford to indulge ourselves because, as former premier Harold Macmillan told us in 1957, slightly paraphrased: 'You've never had it so good'. Not to say we are bereft of ills and misfortunes, far from it; they are there, albeit hidden by that patina that, once buffed away, may reveal a catalogue of discomfiture.

It is how we address those ills that may promulgate our success in society's development; bearing in mind that progress should not be confused with a step in the forward direction. Key to this progress is the usage – and, even more important, the accurate interpretation – of language and its meaning. The current idiom 'Black lives matter' is as curious as it is disquieting since the logical implication of the statement itself is that at some prior point to the catechism they did not. These three words alone

Recorded 16 June 2020

suggest a discourse that is not only a damning critique on what has gone before but which also raises future issues of relative values. 'Lessons will be learnt' is the usual platitude. 'Very little seems to change any time soon' appears to be the reality.

Who of my generation doesn't recall the 'I'm backing Britain' campaign of 1968 – hardly a direct comparison but illustrative nonetheless. Aimed at boosting the British economy it became a nationwide movement within a week. But interest quickly flagged amid much embarrassment and the campaign is now regarded as an iconic example of a failed attempt to transform British thinking.

So, if any movement is to entertain hope of lasting impact it must be commensurate with values, expectations and realities by acting as both a reflector and conductor of a universally desirable set of objectives. It must also, and this is crucial, be delivered in such a way that the message received accurately represents the message sent. It is on this latter aspect that it must be both stated and interpreted correctly and consistently. In this regard we have much to learn from philosophical deliberation and there is one philosopher in particular who springs to mind in encapsulating its significance.

There is a tale about the University scholar who was appraising a student and his PhD thesis. The assessor wasn't particularly enamoured by PhDs, considering them a USA import that had no place in UK academia, so was a trifle jaded from the start. His verdict ran along the lines of: 'This thesis is a work of true genius. It also happens to satisfiy the criteria for a PhD.' The recipient of this glowing backhanded tribute was one Ludwig Josef Johann Wittgenstein (1889–1951) and the subject of the 'genius' epithet was his remarkable *Tractatus Logico-Philosophicus* published in 1921.

At the time of its publication, Wittgenstein concluded that the *Tractatus* had resolved all philosophical problems and he retired from philosophy for many years until realising he had more to offer. His subsequent *Philosphical Investigations*, in which he recanted many of his own earlier assertions in *Tractatus*, did not appear in print until two years after his death.

At a mere seventy five pages *Tractatus* is considered one of the purest distillations of thought ever produced. An aim of the *Tractatus* is to reveal the relationship between language and the world by which Wittgenstein argues that the logical structure of language provides the limits of meaning. A central tenet is his assertion: *Wovon man nicht sprechen kann, darüber muß man schweigen.* Whereof one cannot speak, thereof one must be silent.

Facts and logic are exactly so and can be described; anything beyond these – religion, ethics, aesthetics, the mystical – cannot be rationally discussed and instead require the invocation of feelings, emotions or experiences. They are not of themselves nonsensical, but any statement about them must be, because they cannot be proved or disproved. This view was concurred by his mentor Bertrand Russell who felt that since he could neither prove nor disprove the existence of God he saw no need to even contemplate the question. Russell wrote the introduction to *Tractatus* before he and Wittgenstein developed differences of opinion and became mutually fractious.

The limits of language, for Wittgenstein, are the limits of philosophy. Hence, without apparent hubris, he considered *Tractatus* to be the last word and effectively said we should all pack up and go home. Until he reconsidered.

In a different life as a much younger man part of my daily routine involved presenting principles of accurate and unambiguous §. Recall the days you played Chinese Whispers in the school playground when 'send reinforcements we're going to advance' magically became 'send three and fourpence we're going to a dance' and the problem is self-evident. So how to avoid?

My introduction to Wittgenstein came as a breath of fresh air and though I am not alone in finding his works too challenging to tackle head on – for anyone other than the most gifted student he is all but impenetrable – a heavily edited familiarisation with his basic paradigms, collated by those able to survive the scrum, has proved singularly illuminating.

According to Wittgenstein, language works by words being translated in our brain not by textual recognition but in the form of pictures to which we can relate. The issue is how that picture may vary between the transmitter and the receiver. So, should I tell my other half that I had been chatting in the pub with a young lady I would need to ensure that my entirely innocent exchanges with an office colleague I met there by chance were not misconceived as a clandestine meeting with a secret lover. Or, as we would say in the vernacular, quite literally, 'she might get the wrong picture'. Indeed, she might.

Philosophical Investigations marked a radical departure from the pictures interpretation where Wittgenstein instead referred to 'games theory' in which he postulated that the mind translates aural input into a series of games we use or manipulate in order to translate the messages. So, if I were to say to my other half: 'Don't worry, it will all be OK tomorrow' that simply cannot fall within 'the game of deductions based on fact', since I cannot accurately predict what is going to happen tomorrow. What I am instead playing is 'the game of reasonable expectations based on previous experiences' which is a completely different gambit but with wildly differing potential consequences.

This is a *volte face* from his earlier work but such was his brilliance he claims adherents to both and is still a major influence in contemporary philosophical debate. Check out YouTube for lectures by, say, AC Grayling or Julian Baggini – two modern masters of distilling esoteric academic postulates into digestible brainfood if ever there were – and take it from there; it's fascinating stuff.

But it is most certainly not just for the aesthete or connoisseur and we dismiss such considerations at our peril. Throughout history conflicts have arisen over misunderstandings; even the mythical Trojan War was essentially based on a dubious premise; was Helen of Troy abducted or did she elope?

Wittgenstein alluded to weighty considerations that impinge mightily on our own existences. Of course black lives matter. But by what convoluted strands of warped historical imperatives did we arrive at a position of having to expressly state so? And wherein lie the inbuilt attributes that do not require us to remind ourselves that murder, theft, child abuse or violence are all wrong. Unlike our compliance with imposed constraints of, say, commercial regulations or taxation we should be cognisant by dint of our collective humanity under common law when such as the wilful taking of a life or the oppression of our fellow man are universal wrongs.

In a democracy the people vote for leaders to act by proxy on our behalf; they in turn create the parameters within which we express our views. And how fragile those parameters can be – remind me please, how are things in Hong Kong at the moment? Thus the need for a precision of thought that is underpinned by universal egalitarianism.

There is another aspect that must be factored into our equations, and that is our predilection for opinions and bias which are changeable with time and may, unfortunately, spill over into a panoply of 'isms'. Ingrained beliefs may be difficult to modify despite the strongest counter-argument. They may be suppressed only to re-emerge when the moment is propitious.

As the aforementioned Harold Macmillan is reputed to have once remarked when asked what was most likely to knock governments off course: 'Events, dear boy, events'. No-one saw the coronavirus pandemic coming and Brexit has for the moment taken a back seat. In the meantime, largely but not exclusively fuelled by events beyond our shores we are witnessing a period of civil unrest and widespread malcontent; some peaceful, others not so.

One can but hope that by the time we recover some semblance of virus-free normality this bubbling anger may have muted towards more considered dialogue in which it is acceptable to all that a productive line of address could be established by first levelling the table. I am not convinced there is a global movement for any section of society, be it based on colour, race, religion or sexuality, to be treated more favourably than any another. It is, I contend, more accurate to suggest they would simply all like to be treated the same. To partake in the same game. To be part of the same picture.

And I cannot pass by the irony of my musings here being recorded as a podcast for, as broadcaster Clive Anderson astutely observed during an interview with the *Mail Online* in 2011: 'Radio; it's like TV but the pictures are better'. Ah, perhaps therein lies true acumen.

POSTSCRIPT

USA country music legend and actress Dolly Parton is just one of a number of stars and celebrities moved to offer opinion; this instance is unusual insomuch she rarely comments on politics. In an interview reported in *BBC Online* of 14 August 2020 headed 'Of course Black lives matter' she told Billboard Magazine: 'Do we think our little white a**es are the only ones that matter? No!'

With a broad fan base that spans the right and the left, the singer generally eschews political subjects and is more usually circumspect. In 2017 she remained quiet on stage at the Emmys next to Lily Tomlin and Jane Fonda when her former *9 to 5* co-stars decided to use the spotlight to slam President Trump. This is not the first time the seventy-four-year-old, who is seen as both an LGBT and feminist icon, has supported progressive causes. She came out in favour of gay marriage in 2014, a year before it was legalised nationwide, spoke against anti-transgender 'bathroom bills', and supported the #MeToo movement. But her support for left-leaning issues is usually carefully crafted to be as inoffensive as possible, often urging people to 'judge not lest ye be judged'.

Ms Parton's unobtrusive views may not be quite so familiar to her followers as her more famous putdown quip: 'I'm not offended by all the dumb blonde jokes because I know I'm not dumb ... and I also know that I'm not blonde'.

And in a debate featuring the aforementioned Clive Anderson (*Loose Ends* BBC Radio 4, 28 November 2020) he developed a train of thought that goes some way to answering why specific emphasis is placed on black lives mattering when surely all lives should do so equally. The thrust of his point was that it has long been engrained in Western culture that white lives always have done – hence no requisite for a 'white lives matter' – and that the black lives campaign is necessary to redress the imbalance.

TRACTATUS LOGICO-PHILOSOPHICUS

5.101   The truth-functions of every number of elementary propositions can be written in a schema of the following kind:

$(TTTT)(p, q)$ Tautology (if p then p, and if q then q) $[p \supset p . q \supset q]$
$(FTTT)(p, q)$ in words: Not both p and q. $[\sim(p . q)]$
$(TFTT)(p, q)$ „ „ If q then p. $[q \supset p]$
$(TTFT)(p, q)$ „ „ If p then q. $[p \supset q]$
$(TTTF)(p, q)$ „ „ p or q. $[p \vee q]$
$(FFTT)(p, q)$ „ „ Not q. $[\sim q]$
$(FTFT)(p, q)$ „ „ Not p. $[\sim p]$
$(FTTF)(p, q)$ „ „ p or q, but not both. $[p . \sim q : \vee : q . \sim p]$
$(TFFT)(p, q)$ „ „ If p, then q; and if q, then p. $[p \equiv q]$
$(TFTF)(p, q)$ „ „ p
$(TTFF)(p, q)$ „ „ q
$(FFFT)(p, q)$ „ „ Neither p nor q. $[\sim p . \sim q$ or $p \mid q]$
$(FFTF)(p, q)$ „ „ p and not q. $[p . \sim q]$
$(FTFF)(p, q)$ „ „ q and not p. $[q . \sim p]$
$(TFFF)(p, q)$ „ „ p and q. $[p . q]$
$(FFFF)(p, q)$ Contradiction (p and not p; and q and not q.) $[p . \sim p . q . \sim q]$

Those truth-possibilities of its truth-arguments, which verify the proposition, I shall call its *truth-grounds*.

Extract from the translation of Tractatus Logico-Philosophicus

John Tracy communicates with his father Jeff by videolink from Thunderbird 5, the space station monitor.

PAGES OF TIME

It is said that time moves in mysterious ways; according to Einstein it can even move at different speeds. But how exactly does it move? And does an appreciation of the motion of time offer an insight into conflict resolution? GF explores this from the perspective of Books and Bookmen, *children's television and the after-shocks of a pandemic.*

Many of an age not unadjacent to mine may fondly recall those futuristic puppet series of 1950s and 60s vintage where our childhood daydreams of space travel, underwater exploration and technical wizardry were given life through our string powered wooden heroes.

I was fascinated by the likes of *Thunderbirds* in which Jeff Tracy directed operations from Tracy Island and communicated with his intrepid sons manning Thunderbirds 1 to 5 from the deepest ocean to outer space by way of videolink.

Videolink. Speech and vision over vast distances. Fantastic. Unbelievable.

Such is the march of progress, eh? By the time I reached middle age videolink technology, once the *illusory-provocateur* of a children's television series, now came as bog-standard on my home computer.

And yet I barely used it. Not *blasé* or indifferent – I was keen to – but more of a common notion that despite all this new-fangled stuff you can't beat meeting face to face.

There's nothing like a pandemic to fracture complacency and the Covid-19 scourge, with all that has entailed for social distancing and group gatherings, has not too subtly caused us to completely re-evaluate that one. Sales of video conferencing packages have hit stratospheric levels and it is now the norm across the board, from virtual meetings of family and friends through to corporate undertakings, presentations, lectures, concerts and broadcasting, home teaching; the whole gamut.

And I suspect that, having been nudged across the cyberspace Rubicon, we will not be reverting anytime soon. Me? I welcome it, if only for very practical reasons of time and sheer cost. Until shortly before BC – that's Before Coronavirus – I was routinely undertaking a seven-hour round trip by car, together with the accompanying fuel bills, in appalling traffic congestion and all to offer a meeting little more face-to-face than 'It's in my report'. Lunacy, of which no more. Video it is.

Which brings me to some of the tics, foibles and protocols that have already sprung up around the video conference phenomenon where, by its nature, one is looking at a fellow contributor – or plural – set against a backdrop of their personal environment. And how many of those settings, I have noticed, are shelves of books.

Artificially contrived for the occasion, who knows? It's not just me who suspects; the various radio shows I frequent around the dial now routinely make a point of commenting to the listener how their fellows – whom we, of course, cannot see – are surrounded by books. Whether or not they are, it is all knockabout stuff with sardonic undertones of scholarly pretentiousness. Yet here, notwithstanding the welcome levity, is where I profoundly disagree with the implication that to own and show books is an ostentation; an attempt at trying to look clever.

I believe a good book to be the counterpart of a good friend. You may not have been acquainted very long, you may not know them very well, you may not wish to be at their side all of the while. But when you are together your life is enriched. You wouldn't abuse your friend; you don't deface a book. You don't conceal your friends through awkwardness; you openly display your books without prejudice. And, perhaps most significantly, you may never get to learn all there is to know about your friend, in the same way that it is no shame to admit there are books that you have never finished reading. But you are nonetheless moved by them to the extent that you embrace them as part of your comfort zone.

Hmmm … I'll now lay a small wager that one of the sharper examples of the latter in recent years would be Stephen Hawking's *A Brief History of Time*. First published in 1988 it has sold over twenty-five million copies to date and looks impressive on any bookshelf. Yet I question how many of its purchasers have read it for any distance beyond the first few pages.

Why this is a germane exemplar lies in my confession that not only have I not read it, I haven't even bought it. But I will. It is, to extend my analogy, a future friend I just haven't met yet. I don't know how well I will come to know it, but, presumably much like the twenty-five million who have gone before me, I would value its acquaintance.

One particular book that did come my way recently as a gift from my other half caused me to make the comparison with Hawking. Weighing in at just shy of 400 pages it was destined to keep me occupied for a while so after a couple of deep breaths I decided to put all the other partial-reads to one side and give it a go. I'm glad I did, and the opportunity afforded by enforced time alone enabled me to devour it voraciously. There may not be too many good things to come out of lockdown but this was up there.

How The World Thinks by Julian Baggini is one of those rare tomes that goes way beyond the norm in fundamentally refocussing one's perspectives. I do hope that doesn't sound hyperbole; perhaps it may be less flamboyant to instead say it has channelled – no, crowbarred – my thoughts into new realms of understanding. I have alluded to Baggini elsewhere in my deliberations and, on the strength of this, I will likely do so again.

Dr Julian Baggini is Academic Director of the Royal Institute of Philosophy, the author of several other books and a regular correspondent for national magazines, periodicals and think-tanks. Notwithstanding his evident intellect, the appeal of *How The World*

Thinks is its sheer accessibility aided considerably by an elegant syntax that hits the minimalist bulls-eye with a combination of unerring accuracy and graceful efficiency.

Take this, for example, in his digest of Part 1: 'I hope', he says, 'that it is now obvious why I have started this book by asking how the world *knows*. It might at first look like an abstract question, but if we want to understand how the world *thinks* it is fundamental. It helps one to be better prepared to understand ideas about how the world *is*.' Gosh. I wish I'd written that.

One section that especially caught my eye – which doesn't really narrow it down because they all did – is Baggini's exposition on time. Hawking examined time, too. But Hawking was a scientist, Baginni is a philosopher. Entire volumes have been given to explaining the distinction so forgive my condescending clumsiness in thinking I can do so in one sentence, but here goes: Philosophy is the quest for knowledge by logical thought in questioning the nature of the universe; science is the establishing of facts by data-driven observation.

Hawkings' conclusions? Take another look at his book; there's twenty-five million out there somewhere that will give the low-down on his empiricism. And Baginni? Well, he explores the quite mind-expanding distinction between *linear* and *circular* time. The *what*?

In Christian society we are accustomed to thinking of time in a straight line, specifically yesterday, today and tomorrow. This is reinforced by a religious doctrine of life itself along a course from birth, through the now and to our eventual death. We have considered this as a default for our faith in progress lying in the forward direction since the age of the Enlightenment.

Conversely some cultures, notably those who rely on oral tales and folklore as evidence of identity, believe their history 'goes full circle' and must be passed on through the generations for its sense of place to survive. In direct contradiction to the Book of Revelation that describes Jesus as 'Alpha and Omega, the beginning and the end, the first and the last', Alpha and Omega are at one and the same point; the beginning is the end, the first is the last.

The circle may not retain the same dimension but may expand as time progresses through successive generations. In some Middle East paradigms there is a hybrid of the linear and cyclical. Islamic conceptions of time are as cycles based on appearances of prophets but which develop linearly by moving humanity forward towards the ultimate revelation signified by the judgement-day events associated with the appearance of the *Mahdi*. In Chinese cyclical thought wisdom and truth are timeless and we do not need so much to go forward as to hold on to that we already have. Confucius believed that his purpose 'was not to announce any new truths or initiate any new economy' but was 'to prevent that which is already known from being lost.'

Whilst such divergences from our concept of linear time may be difficult to grasp they are a prerequisite to us understanding the likes of Maori *ethos* and Aboriginal 'dream-time'.

Most of us would be hard pushed to identify our own metaphysical framework, that is, our personal understanding of the structure of nature, but we all have one and, without realising it, unconsciously base our assumptions and values on tenets that have been instilled in us generationally. And, as Baginni suggests, it is by bringing these assumptions to the surface that we may also better understand how other peoples, not of our persuasion, see the world and why they see it that way. It is, as he concludes with commendable clarity: 'Sometimes, simply by changing the frame, the whole picture can look very different.'

Now, let us cut to the chase; does that not sound like an elucidation of the root cause of centuries of war and conflict across the globe? And does it not also offer a pragmatic contemporary roadmap towards resolution in just about every one being played out right now? It certainly did for the South African Truth and Reconciliation Commission, which was founded on a conciliatory recognition of widely divergent standpoints following the collapse of Apartheid.

There is a thoughtful scene in an otherwise grim psychological murder movie *Seven*, released in 1995 and starring Brad Pitt alongside Morgan Freeman, where Freeman is researching late at night in a library. He notices a group of night-security personnel idling and queries why, surrounded by a world of knowledge at their fingertips, they choose to play cards. A quarter of a century later when they might instead be video-chatting with their mates, let's hazard a guess at where they would position the laptop camera. *Apropos* my earlier rebuttal of the implication that to own and show books is an ostentation; an attempt at trying to look clever, I am willing to concede exceptions.

The demise of the printed word has been predicted almost from the day that William Caxton's press ground into life in the late fifteenth century. Yet despite our monumental technological advancements since then books are still around in some abundance. Notably, it now seems, on videolinks. Long may it continue, if only for me envisaging certain conceptual difficulties in making friends with a hard drive.

POSTSCRIPT

Presenter Sarah Smith (*Today* BBC Radio 4 dated 29 August 2020) reports on …

'A spy thriller in which the hero has to try and stop the outbreak of WWIII is the film that hopes to tempt us all back into cinemas. It's called *Tenet* and it is a film with a twist because time can go backwards as well as forwards; bullets can reverse their way back into a gun. Now if you think that sounds outlandish you might be intrigued to know that the Director Christopher Nolan was inspired by very real aspects of theoretical physics.'

Smith then goes on to interview Carlo Rovelli, an Italian theoretical physicist and author of *The Order of Time* who describes the theoretical possibility of time going backwards. 'This is the fact that the past and the future are much less different from one another in the real world than what we usually think about. The difference between the past and the future is more an issue of perspective and probability than real actual physical difference.'

Alpha and Omega symbology at Clervaux Abbey, Luxembourg

Oscar Wilde trial at the Old Bailey

WALKING THE WALK

In a variation of the eternal nature-nurture debate, whether determined by personal preference or genetic disposition, we all have our own direction of travel through life. No two paths are the same and some are not so smooth as others, but perhaps there may be a utopian option that may help us all attain the same destination of communal harmony. GF explores the options.

Recently on one glorious summer Saturday, noting that the day had indeed commenced with the promise of 'set fair' as indicated on my barometer, I submitted to *carpe diem* and seized the opportunity of tending the lawn. There being quite a lot of said lawn I tackled it all in the one session instead of over the more usual two and was rewarded with the muscle aches to prove it. So, with the other various human and animal occupants of *Chez-moi* idling in their own secret somewheres I felt I had earnt a bit of me-time with my feet up. Add a large glass of America's finest cask-strength Bourbon and I, too, was 'set fair'.

Regular followers of my ramblings will know my home is devoid of TV. Lob an arm in any direction and you will connect with either a cat or a radio. So, adjusting the tuning dial on one of the cats I stumbled across some station or other playing 'oldies'. Track of the moment was Lou Reed's *Walk on the Wild Side* from 1972.

The reason my ears pricked up at this gritty urban portrait describing a series of individuals on their way to New York, with its visceral references to then-taboo subjects including transvestites, male prostitution, drugs and sexual practises, is that it whisked me back to that same year, 1972, and a similarly sunny Saturday in the north of England during my undergraduate days. I was never what one would call a gifted student and was covetous of my fellows who could suck in knowledge as if through a straw. The attainment of my modest clutch of qualifications necessitated much time-consuming graft woven in a matrix of frustration at my intellectual inadequacies. The amount of hair I pulled out; I wonder I am not bald. But a lazy Saturday afternoon was one luxury I granted myself, if only to recharge the batteries and stay sane.

There I was in the refectory where I noticed a solitary man seated at a table despite numerous other people sitting disinterestedly at other tables nearby. He looked lonely, so I asked if I could join him. 'Please do' he replied softly, 'I'm Howard'.

Let me describe Howard. Mid-20s, chisel-featured, ascetically thin but finely

Recorded 25 July 2020

proportioned, I guess he would have nudged way over six feet tall in his stockinged toes and his long flaxen locks hung over expensively attired shoulders. He was languidly puffing on a long churchwarden pipe and as the wisps of smoke wafted past his cheeks I couldn't avoid noticing that his eyes, fixed in the middle distance, were twin pools of sadness. We sat quietly for some minutes before I broke the silence and enquired if he was OK. He heaved a sigh of despair, looked me in the eye and poured out: 'I am heartbroken. My boyfriend has just left me'.

How upsetting is that? Howard, you see, was the Chair of the local group of what was then known as the Gay Liberation Front. It all fell into place. Students may assume polarised political views but they are, in my experience, generally libertarian in personal attitudes. Thus, whilst I am not aware that Howard was victimised for his sexuality – as was prevalent in the big bad world beyond the comfort zone of academia – I am prepared to accept that those, quite literally, on the outside were oblivious to his angst and simply did not know how to react. Perhaps, and I do not criticise them for their ignorance, they didn't even try and instead just chose to walk on the other side. I understand there's a story in the Bible that runs along similar lines.

Howard and I chatted until well into late afternoon. I never saw him again but that one meeting educated the youthful me in just how desperately isolated some people can feel simply because they are what they are.

The mind doth work in curious ways and no sooner had I remembered Howard I linked to memories of a man from the same era, George whom I worked alongside in my holidays – 'to earn a bit of bread, man' – and I still reel at his pain when this dignified and unassumingly quintessential English businessman learnt that his son was a transvestite and suspected homosexual.

His spirit was broken more than his pride and shortly afterwards, although not recorded as such on his certificate, George died of shame.

Fast-forward to half a century later where we do not bat an eyelid at the likes of comedian Eddie Izzard and artist Grayson Perry who are known as much for their feminine attire as they are for their talents. Such once-debauched conduct is fêted, with the Gay Pride movement embracing lesbians, gays, transvestites, bisexuals, transsexuals, non-binary, non-identifying and more in a cornucopia of those declaring an alternative lifestyle. There will surely come a time when the term 'alternative' becomes an irrelevance and everything becomes part of the mainstream because, well, everything *is* mainstream.

Since my naive encounter with Howard I now revel in the company of numerous gay friends and family members happy to declare their sexuality in feeling similarly unthreatened. Lest we forget, there are countries and cultures that lag way behind us in acceptance and, in an increasingly globalised world, therein lies a challenge. It is not insurmountable; it may just take time. One hundred and twenty-five years after *The love that dare not speak its name* – a phrase from the 1892 poem *Two Loves* by Lord Alfred Douglas – was pejoratively cited at Oscar Wilde's trial, that very same love is now recognised, acknowledged, rejoiced and celebrated.

Within the Grand Scheme of social evolution this is a speedy transformation. It was only in 1967 that the Sexual Offences Act repealed elements of sexual criminality; not all, but it was a start. Though the trend is progressive it is not a perfect process and there are occasional stutters. The provisions of 'Section 28' of the Local Government Act 1988 – widely described at the time as a step backwards – sought to ban the 'promotion' of homosexuality by local authorities and in Britain's schools. 'Promotion', as used by the Thatcher government, was a contentious word, more accurately the clause meant in practise that teachers were effectively barred from discussing same-sex relationships with students and councils were forbidden from stocking libraries with literature or films that contained gay or lesbian themes. Amidst tumultuous opposition the clause was repealed, first in Scotland and then England. In 2009 David Cameron apologised for Clause 28 and admitted it had been 'a mistake'.

A contemporary example of attempts to reconcile opposing views is panning out under public gaze at the very moment I am writing this, whereby the Scottish government is deliberating over a piece of legislation seeking to criminalise allegedly offensive language against minorities, including personal opinion and satire, as a hate crime. Depending on one's view, this is either a safeguarding of those minorities' rights or a grotesque attack on free speech and humour. There's just no absolute answer to that dichotomy and, as usual, a compromise will probably lie somewhere down the middle. But these examples do illustrate the difficulties in reaching a resolution, and what may happen when the resolution itself be thrust into obsolescence as society's own attitudes change.

There is a difference between reparation and re-writing history. Much as we may be tempted to remove unsavoury chapters from our past – there is no nation on earth that does not have its dark chapters – to eradicate them from future recountings would not only be a travesty of the truth, it would also deny us the opportunity to learn from those mistakes and modify our attitudes accordingly. As the novelist and philosopher George Santayana put it succinctly: 'Those who cannot remember the past are condemned to repeat it'.

We should be catholic in accepting our mistakes and refer to them as a springboard to inform our future actions. We cannot do this if they are erased from history. It is now considered monstrous that the genius mathematician Alan Turing, he of Bletchley Park code-breaking fame, should have elected chemical castration rather than prison – what a choice, eh? – for submitting to 'the love that dare not speak its name'. Try to imagine the torment of the man who felt his best option was to swallow a cyanide capsule in 1954 aged just forty-one. His pardon by Prime Minister Gordon Brown in 2009 for 'the appalling way he was treated'

The new £50 note issued 23 June 2021
featuring Alan Turing on the reverse

could, of course never bring Turing back. But the recognition of the historical facts does help alter the trajectory of our route along the never-ending path to ultimate social enlightenment. Not merely a step forward but genuine progress.

And so, after fifty years of liberation, changes in law, public displays, pressure groups, characters and celebrities in which the whole scene has gone totally *volte face* from Wilde's time of incarceration in Reading Gaol, I was saddened to hear recently of a celebrated footballer who, despite his trappings of fame and wealth, admitted to missing the companionship because he is afraid of revealing he is gay.

Justin Fashanu was the first black professional footballer to openly proclaim being gay way back in 1990 and although he paid a terrible price for his admission – the note accompanying his suicide in 1998 was testament to his distress – after three decades his coming out no longer sets any precedent. Yet here in 2020 there are still those whom, for whatever reason, are fearful of the consequences of revealing themselves simply because they are what they are. Why must our fellows, of any sexual orientation, feel tormented to the extent they take their own lives?

My overarching question is; why does it still matter when in the final analysis it is a purely personal consideration that is nobody else's business. My answer – or should I say my fervent hope – is that it will eventually diminish to the point that it does not. Looking beyond the gay scene, that same question and answer session applies equally to the catalogue of society's current ailments; racism, sexism, religious intolerance, ageism *etcetera, etcetera, etcetera.* When we strike the balance of equating the inadequacies of our past with using them to constructively inform our future a natural and logical consequence will be that they all will cease to be an issue.

In the pursuit of that utopia, more aspirational than practical I admit but it is our civic duty to try, we have a long way to go and it is in the nature of the human condition that there are those who choose alternative routes. Should forbearance and tolerance continue to grow then it will be to our universal good fortune that all sides get less wild by the day.

And on that optimistic reflection I would like to dedicate this piece in memory of songwriter Lou Reed who embarked on his own last *Walk on the Wild Side* when he died of liver complications on 27 October 2013 aged seventy-one.

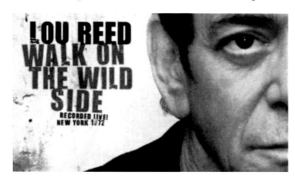

POSTSCRIPT

It begs the question: 'When will we ever learn?' This, from *The Independent Online* dated 21 July 2020 (sixteen days after this podcast was first recorded) …

New Zealand Prime Minister Jacinda Ardern has 'vowed to ban conversion therapy' if her party returns to power, as is widely expected to happen in the country's upcoming election on 17 October. *(The governing Labour Party led by incumbent Ardern won in a landslide victory against the National Party led by Judith Collins – author)*

'It is a practice that causes harm and is out of place in the kind, inclusive and modern country we are' said party leader Tāmati Coffey.

This adds New Zealand to the growing list of countries looking to outlaw conversion therapy, including Canada, Chile, Mexico and Germany (Brazil, Ecuador and Malta already have bans in place). But in Britain it is still happening, despite the government pledging to ban it.

The term 'conversion therapy' covers a range of practises that falsely claim to change a person's sexual orientation, gender identity or expression. The practise is based on an assumption that being lesbian, gay, bi or trans is a mental illness that can be 'cured'.

Despite all major UK therapy professional bodies and the NHS rejecting it and stating that it is dangerous, some practitioners continue to conduct conversion therapy. In 2018, the government pledged to ban conversion therapy. On 20 July (UK Prime Minster) Boris Johnson described gay conversion therapy as 'absolutely abhorrent' and said it 'has no place in a civilised society, has no place in this country'.

'What we are going to do is a study right now on, you know, where is this actually happening, how prevalent is it, and we will then bring forward plans to ban it' he said.

In response to his comments, the Ban Conversion Therapy campaign said: 'We're delighted that Boris Johnson has listened to our calls for a ban on conversion therapy'.

And from *BBC Online* dated 9 March 2021:
Campaigners have accused the government of not moving quickly enough towards banning LGBT+ 'conversion therapy' in England and Wales.

MPs from across the political spectrum called during a Westminster debate for the practice to be made illegal. Equalities minister Kemi Badenoch said the government was committed to ending it, and took the issue very seriously. But equality campaigners and some MPs said targeted action was needed. Conversion therapy refers to any form of treatment or psychotherapy which aims to change a person's sexual orientation or gender identity, ranging from electric shock treatment to religious teaching and discussion. The practice is already outlawed in Switzerland and parts of Australia, Canada and the US …

Boris Johnson said in July that the practice was 'absolutely abhorrent' and that plans for a ban would be brought forward. The government commissioned research into the ban – which was first proposed by Theresa May in 2018 – but ministers have yet to publish details. Responding to the Westminster Hall debate, Ms Badenoch said: 'I want to assure you that we are committed to ending conversion therapy in the UK and we take this issue very seriously. This practice has no place in civilised society'.

"ALSO, THE BRIDGE IS OUT AHEAD"
(smallest text at the bottom)

MAD OR BAD?

Health and safety, a cornerstone of modern industrial practise since 1974, still attracts more than its fair share of ridicule. But is its denigration justified, and on what evidence do its detractors base their belittlement? GF takes a look from the perspective of a novel accolade.

The Darwin Awards, named after the eponymous Charles Robert Darwin, an English naturalist best known for his contributions to the science of evolution, are tongue-in-cheek honours conferred – often posthumously – on those who, by their actions, have de-selected themselves out of the gene pool by death or sterility. The term 'survival of the fittest' – often incorrectly attributed to Darwin – was coined by Herbert Spencer (1809–1903), a brilliant polymath and contemporary of Darwin. After reading his *On the Origin of Species* Spencer first used the phrase 'survival of the fittest' in his *Principles of Biology* (published 1864), in which he drew parallels between his own economic theories and Darwin's biological one: 'This survival of the fittest, which I have here sought to express in mechanical terms, is that which Mr Darwin has called 'natural selection', or the preservation of favoured races in the struggle for life.'

Fitness as applied to natural selection is defined as the degree of success in reproduction. This is primary. Albeit we are top of the evolutionary tree – for now, that is – if we strip away our *mores*, culture, philanthropy, aesthetics, history and our inflated sense of self-worth, the sole purpose of human endeavour is to continue the species by reproduction. If that one endeavour fails then all else becomes an irrelevance. Because we will be extinct.

Should mankind eventually muddle its way to oblivion – which, let's be honest, is attracting increasingly shorter odds – then there are those who consider it possible that the ensuing dominant species may be insects and small invertebrates. A bold proposition, yet the evidence is persuasive.

Consider our limitations; first our diet. Over a period of just a few thousand years our digestive system has specialised to the extent that we cannot readily digest uncooked meat. The appendix, now vestigial and unnoticed except for when it becomes inflamed, once allowed us to digest cellulose. Hence, unlike many insects who still have the requisite enzymes in their digestive tract, we have long lost the ability to graze on wood.

Our reproduction involves a mammalian placental system that although protecting the unborn safely inside the mother involves a gestation of nine months to produce at very most a handful of offspring at a time.

Recorded 28 August 2020

Our body temperature regulation mechanism means that without suitable clothing we are quickly prone to hypothermia at -10°C and uncomfortably hot above 30°C, giving us a puny survival range of just 40°C.

Compare and contrast with insects and small invertebrates; their ability to eat an extensive array of matter, to survive long-term in extremes of temperature from the Arctic to Death Valley and, most importantly, to reproduce in vast numbers in short order make them prime candidates to successfully continue their species in a post-apocalyptic world devoid of humans. Here's food for thought, quite literally; in the immediate aftermath following the bombing of Hiroshima, cockroaches were found grazing in the rubble directly adjacent to ground zero.

Meanwhile, back at the Darwin awards ...

These recognize individuals most of whom, it has to be said, are moronic and whose demise by their sheer idiocy would be purple sad were it not so humorous. By self-removal, or so the theory goes, one more fruit loop is eliminated from the gene pool thereby rendering it more fit for purpose as the progenitor for succeeding generations.

All good knockabout stuff; let's look a few recent examples who have graced the ranks:

* In 2019 American Ronald Cyr shot himself dead when he forgot that he had installed a device for firing a gun at anyone who opened his door without invitation. He opened the door.

* In 2018 New Zealander Howard Miller, an experienced welder, inexplicably chose to mix his separate oxygen and acetylene supplies into the one tank. A deadly combination, no sooner he lit his nozzle than the flame went backwards into the tank and exploded. Thoughtfully, he had also decided to weld adjacent to a store of spirit cleaner. The resultant fireball destroyed houses for several blocks around and left little trace of Howard.

* And finally, to mercilessly hammer the point, in 2018 two Polish men were involved in a minor collision on a main road. The ensuing argument led to a brawl that spread into the middle of the busy highway where both were oblivious to the oncoming truck.

Originating in newsgroups sometime around 1985 the Darwin Awards were formalised in 1993 as a website where visitors can vote for their favourite candidate, and the publication of several books. Both elements were instigated by one Wendy Northcutt, a graduate in molecular biology from the University of California, Berkeley. The site has attracted its share of imitators and many of the unconfirmed stories purporting to be Darwinian are urban myths. Hence the rules of the Darwin Awards insist that verification is key. Alas, the awards have not noticeably helped diminish the propensity for humanity to act idiotically.

No matter how many rules and regulations are invoked aimed at preserving life or preventing injury there will always be someone who feels they know better, with catastrophic results. It is impossible to fully protect the foolish from themselves but visionary legislators and philanthropists have still defied the odds in their efforts to do so, notably in the struggle against what they see as rogue industrialists.

Acts accommodating factories, mines, explosives and employers liabilities have been around for centuries but arguably one of the most contentious contributions in recent years was the all-embracing *Health and Safety At Work Act* of 1974. Contentious because it polarised opinion between those on the safety side who felt it was a landmark in protecting workers and placing obligations on employers to create a safe working environment, and the detractors who saw it as an unashamed extension of the nanny-state. I also suspect an input of macho-fuelled rebellion whereby the kudos of 'doing the job the tough old way' was threatened and an inflexibility promulgated by a wariness of what these interfering busybodies will come up with next. Such as:

Children being banned from playing conkers unless they wear goggles
Office workers banned from putting up Christmas decorations
Trapeze artists having to wear hard hats
Pin the tail on the donkey declared a safety risk
Banning candy floss on a stick

All, and many more, cited by critics of Health and Safety as serious infringements of our liberties. And all entirely false.

In a classic exposition of an inaccuracy travelling half way around the world before a truth has got its boots on, it is impossible to trace where some of these baffling myths originate. But they all have one crucial thing in common – they are most emphatically not enshrined in health and safety law.

Unsurprisingly the overseeing Health and Safety Executive are not impressed. 'There are few greater myths than that health and safety has gone mad' says the executive. 'We've debunked some truly ridiculous misrepresentations of health and safety, including the banning of conkers and firemen's poles. We've scotched scare stories about excessive safety signs, rebutted rumours about onerous risk assessments and kicked back at claims that kids need to be wrapped in cotton wool. This trivialisation concerns us. It confuses businesses about their responsibilities and workers about their rights.'

Now, in my efforts to remain impartial I am finding this a bit of a tricky one. I consider myself a libertarian but conversely recognise the need to insulate the ill-prepared from themselves – which, I accept, sometimes might include me. But do we achieve this from legislation or education? Ah, I submit it is a combination of both. Many life skills are accrued as a consequence of one's upbringing; principally under the tutelage of parents or peers. So where does one draw the line between formal education and informal cognizance?

Do I really need advice that a twenty feet tall rickety ladder leaning perilously against a wall may not be safe to ascend? There are those who choose to take the risk rather than err on the side of caution and for them, well, it is back to the Darwin Awards.

It must be said that sometimes the imperative for legislation may be a result of a self-fulfilling prophecy or for reasons one could not have envisaged. CJD (mad cow disease) and, more recently, Coronavirus are the consequences of our interference in what hitherto had been a settled order of nature.

I do not come to bury Health and Safety nor do I come to praise it but I do offer a defence of common sense and basic education. Our health and our safety clearly requires a regulatory framework yet I contend this has often overstepped the mark into the territory of personal responsibility, to the detriment of our initiative.

It is the actions of zealots or the over-cautious that grate on the sensitivities and it may be easier to defray something on the specious excuse that H&S legislation does not permit it. Oh, how often have I endured committees where creativity has been stifled at birth on the spurious grounds of contravening safety rather than formulating a risk assessment that identifies the hazards and presents practical solutions to mitigating them.

This attitude has led to a near-universal epidemic of risk aversion to the point of madness, although it is not aided by a compensation culture of 'where there's blame there's a claim'. It is this over-the-top caveat that belittles the true health and safety message and I have some random examples in front of me that I find especially irksome.

Let's take a look; first of all I have a packet of peanuts, the labelling of which declares 'Contents, nuts, salt' … etc, you get the picture. So far, so good. Until we come to the bit that states 'This product may contain nuts.' Really? What else was I expecting? And am I so ill-informed to need to be told 'Contents bleach. Do not drink'. But my favourite for now is a leaflet that I found inside a water bottle I recently purchased. It is written in no fewer than six languages and contains the usual advice on not putting it in a microwave, only wash it in soapy water and so on. Fair enough, until I get to the bottom of this lengthy multilingual liturgy and see: 'Entrapment hazard – do not stick tongue down bottle neck. Injury can result.'

Now come on, no amount of legislation and advice is going to prevent some buffoon, for reasons best known to themselves, doing exactly that. But it doesn't mean we shouldn't try. Because they're out there; an entire cabal going out of their way to give common sense and reasonable precaution a bad name. So, stop and think. It may be dangerous. Apparently. But if you must, then take solace that the honour of a Darwin Award could soon be all yours. Enjoy. And may those you leave behind continue to procreate.

POSTSCRIPT

It is difficult to better this for pointless inanity that has come to light since the recording of the podcast. The location unspecified but it is evidently genuine. As in any other walk of life, Health and Safety attracts its zealots. But it's a fair bet there's someone out there who has cut their fingers on the edge. Or gone over the bridge.

www.darwinAwards.com
History & Rules

In the spirit of Charles Darwin, the Darwin Awards commemorate individuals who protect our gene pool by making the ultimate sacrifice of their own lives. Darwin Award winners eliminate themselves in an extraordinarily idiotic manner, thereby improving our species' chances of long-term survival.

History

In his seminal work, "The Origin of Species," Charles Darwin presented evidence that species evolve over time to fit their environment better. Do the Darwin Awards really represent examples of human evolution in action?

Consider that there are three requirements for evolution to occur. First, a species must show diversity. For example, some people are taller than others. Second, there must be a selective pressure working on this trait. If people live among trees, and tall people whack their heads on branches and kill themselves more frequently than their shorter fellows, then short people will have a survival advantage. Third, the trait must be inheritable. On average, short people have shorter children than tall people, so evolution favors short people in this example. Within a few generations, our species would become shorter, and it would also become better at evading low branches.

The stories on this website, which range from the sublimely ironic to the pathetically stupid, display examples of trial and (fatal) error that vividly illustrate evolution in all its selective glory.

I started collecting the stories that make up the Darwin Awards in 1993, while I was doing biological research at Stanford University. I found them in newspaper articles from around the world and once I verified their legitimacy, I rewrote them for a small mailing list of friends. As people passed these emails around, I began to receive nominations from far and wide. When the Stanford server became overloaded, I moved the pages to www.DarwinAwards.com, set up voting and submission mechanisms, and became the primary source of and repository for the Darwin Awards.

Through word-of-mouth, as well as my email newsletter, the website has attracted a huge following. The dark humor, engaging stories, and mordant social commentary have made the Darwin Awards one of the most popular humor sites on the web.

Rules

So how are the Darwin Awards actually determined?

Nominees significantly improve the gene pool by eliminating themselves from the human race in an obviously stupid way. They are self-selected examples of the dangers inherent in a lack of common sense, and all human races, cultures, and socioeconomic groups are eligible to compete. Actual winners must meet the following criteria:

Reproduction
The prime tenet of the Darwin Awards is that we are celebrating the self-removal of incompetent genetic material from the human race. Therefore, the potential winner must be deceased, or at least incapable of reproducing.

Excellence
The candidate must suffer an astounding lapse of judgement. It takes a phenomenal failure of common sense to earn a Darwin Award. Common idiocies like Russian Roulette are not sufficient to win this dubious distinction.

Self-Selection
The candidate must be the cause of his own demise. The candidate's own gross ineptitude must be the cause of the incident that earns him the nomination.

Maturity
The candidate must be capable of sound judgement.

Veracity
The event must be verified.

Abridged extract from www.darwinawards.com

The Macallan New Distillery and Visitors Experience

A BETTER WAY

Can scientific advancements trump good old-fashioned human knowledge and experience? GF examines the issue from the perspective of an appreciation of Uisge Beatha, the Gaelic 'water of life'.

Auntie Beeb does it on Radio 4; why shouldn't I? So, here's my thought for the day; does science always hold all the answers?

Now, I'll just let that one burble in the background whilst I expand upon my reservations …

If I have lusted over a lifetime in cultivating my passion for epicurean pleasures then there is one that been my mistress since I was 18 years old. Ah, how I recall the first time I fell for the seduction of *Uisge*, as it is spelt in Gaelic, or as we more usually refer to it, whisky. More specifically, malt whisky. Allow me to explain both the circumstances and the distinction.

There I was enjoying one Friday evening with my dear late father – we were like brothers and Friday was 'our evening' – when we ventured into The Britannia, an Inn close to what was then home, and sought a tipple of something a bit different from the usual fayre to titivate our palates. 'Ever had one of these?' enquired our genial host, pointing to a bottle labelled Blair Atholl. Dad and I sipped a nip each and glanced at each other euphorically as our eyes rolled heavenward in sheer pleasure. Here was unalloyed hedonism, unbridled decadence, quintessential bliss, all in a glass. And from that, you may gather, we were smitten.

Mine host gently prodded into our reveries and explained this was 'proper' whisky, reserved on the top shelf for the connoisseur, not the mass-produced blended stuff held upside down on the optics. As an aside, this was our first experience of pure Scottish malt whisky from the only bottle of pure Scottish malt whisky on the premises since in those days few made their way much past the border. How things have changed in the interim, where my local corner shop now has an entire shelf buckling under the stuff, but back to my tale. Mine host explained that unlike, say, vodka that can be enjoyed as soon as it emerges from the still, whisky has to be made under strictly controlled circumstances and, as he poetically intoned 'not a drop can be sold 'til it is three years old'. We knew he wasn't kidding, it was written on the bottle.

Well, that did it for me and I was – excuse the pun – intoxicated; fascinated by this magical potion. So, to cut to the chase, I put my nose to the grindstone, did my homework and within a short time thereafter had written several articles, droned on interminably to anyone who would listen about my investiture and compiled a presentation – in those days on overhead acetate projection slides – that I hawked around decades before the advent of computerised PowerPoint.

The intervening years have seen me undertake visits to manifold distilleries and – joy upon joy – for a 'significant birthday' (my sixtieth) my good lady took me on a trip to become intimate with several of my mistresses as together she and I undertook masterclasses on every distillery on Islay, off the west coast of Scotland and home to my favourite brands. Fate also played its part and when we relocated to the Welsh border we found ourselves just a few miles from the Penderyn distillery in the Brecons. Its tale, and a fascinating one at that involving a descendant of the founding father of electricity Michael Faraday who made the unique still, is for another time; but it was following another visit there just a few days ago coupled with an item I coincidentally heard on the news that spurred me to reminisce.

GF enjoying the masterclass at the Caol Ila distillery, Islay

Before I do ruminate further about an alcoholic quaff there are those who might suggest I should offer the usual caveats of drinking responsibly *etcetera, etcetera* but, to the genuine *aficionado*, this would seem somewhat incongruous. To partake in an appreciation session is akin to being a member of a devout order; there is a tranquillity and reverence for the Holy Spirit. A glass containing the merest dampening is first swirled in the base and observed for clarity, brilliance, sparkle, colour and depth. Depending on the strength – commercial whisky is sold at 40 degrees proof, 'cask strength' may be approaching 70 – there may be discussion as to whether it requires 'cutting' by the addition of fresh spring water or sampled neat. No ice, please; the temperate shock can radically affect the compounds. Sacrilege, in my opinion. But then again, though purists may disagree, I tend there is no right or wrong way on how to enjoy your snifter and I have engaged in many a debate with them on the merits of that one aspect alone.

Whatever, malt whisky is the only spirituous liquor known to man in the which the addition of water entirely transforms the perception. Try it for yourself. Pour a shot of gin and put water in it. Result? It tastes of watered-down gin. Now consider, let's say one of my favourites sitting on my shelf right now, a 12-year old Caol Ila. On its own this is a robust cask strength spirit reeking heavily of carbolic and phenols. Put it into a shot-glass in which just the teensiest measure of spring water has been swilled around and thrown out, leaving just a residue on the wall and wow! Smell it – 'nosing', it's called, and see if you agree with the accompanying tasting notes that suggest:

Fresh, herbal. Rubbed peppermint leaves, stemmy, damp grass, smoky. Oily, cigar leaves, smoked ham, hickory. Lemon peel at the harbour.

Lemon peel at the harbour? What? It's a very intimate, personal thing is this whisky tasting. Which is it's allure. Swallowing the stuff seems almost ancillary since it only confirms what you have already gathered from the look and the nose. But if you do elect to roll the majestic liquescent gently around the mouth and onwards towards the throat those same notes suggest:

Palate: Good body, oily, tar, elegant smoke. Hints of boiled sweets.
Finish: Long, peppery, spicy warmth, smoke.

A bottle of this quality could set you back hundreds of pounds northwards so the last thing you'll want to do is gluttonously over-imbibe. Hence no need for nanny-state sobriety caveats; one is hardy likely to have a night out on the town swigging it indiscriminately.

The real deal, eh? What's the difference? Well, the secret of whisky goes back to the days when the heavenly liquid was distilled in pot-shaped vessels hidden away from the loathed excise man. 'Rabbie' Burns was once one such, and before becoming better remembered as the Scottish Bard he unknowingly walked across the town centre over concealed pot-stills on his way to work.

The time-honoured pot still of Celtic lore was laborious and worked on one batch in/ one batch out. The arrival of the Patent, or Coffey, still named after Aeneas Coffey, an inventor born in Dublin in 1780 and who, like Burns, was once a 'Surveyor of Excise', heralded the era of mass production. Ireland was a world leader in whisky making; the Coffey still was an arrangement of two fractionating columns from which spirit could be produced continuously and its introduction to Scotland had a profound effect on the indigenous industry.

Seeking to capitalise on a combination of pot-still quality and Coffey-still efficiency, the enterprising Mr Davidge mixed the two brews together and sold the product as Scotch whisky. He picked the wrong fight and the uproar from the industry in Scotland was as predictable as it was tumultuous. It led to the *Royal Commission on Whisky and other potable spirits of 1908* which set the standard in a law that is still extant. In essence, it defines Scotch Whisky as 'a diastase of saccharified malted barley distilled in Scotland and matured in oak barrels for a period of not less than three years'.

Note this is Scotch whisky; let me not digress into the difference between this and that produced elsewhere, why whisky is sometimes spelt with an 'e', or how its expression – i.e. its age and proof – and its manufacture varies. The Japanese can't get enough of the stuff and a testament to their ingenuity in producing it is the range of excellent spirits that are a long way down yonder from their production in the 1970s of a little-lamented marque named *King Anne*. But to be called *Scotch Malt Whisky* it has to be aged for at least three years in oak barrels, and it has to be made in Scotland. That's the law.

Thinking back, I can't recall tasting many Scotch malt whiskies that are just three years old; those that I do I remember were light, precocious affairs. But, as always, it is a question of personal preference. Ditto the variation between Highland, Lowland, and Island that is readily identifiable to even the most innocent of taste buds. To offer an idea, imagine a line drawn from Greenock to Dundee; anything below is a Lowland and above is a Highland. Look at the terrain on a map and note how the lowland hints at a soft heathery background whilst the highland is indicative of a hardier offspring.

The Island malts – my darlings – are robust to the point of being almost chewable and are characteristically denoted by the smack of peaty soil and salt-tanged air of the rugged coastline. The differences between whiskies are sublime and, for sure, there is a malt to match every inclination.

The time spent in the barrel is what defines the depth and character and something between seven and twenty-five years is preferable. Anything over thirtyfive years may be subject to deterioration, and there is always the loss by evaporation through the wood – the 'Angel's Share'. And no, it doesn't mature in the bottle.

Ah, but enough; how could I endlessly wax lyrical about this spirit that has given me so much pleasure for so many years and of which James Hogg, the Ettrick Shepherd said; 'thence to the belly the fire passes; clearly it was not water I had drunk, it was life'.

So, as to my initial postulate: Does science always hold all the answers?

Well, listening to my radio this very morning I hear that scientists have discovered a method to evaluate a whisky's provenance by way of laser analysis. Counterfeit whisky has become big business but similarly a genuine whisky can wane over time rendering it of considerably lesser value. Hence the long-sought imperative for a means of assay which now, thanks to the wonderful advancements of science, can be analysed and quantified by means of laser analysis through the bottle. *Et voilà*, the composition can be identified and the quality can be assessed without so much as popping a cork.

All very impressive, I am sure. But, reflecting on a lifetime of active research as I reach for my favourite Stourbridge crystal decanter and hand-cut tumbler, I think I know a much better way.

Cheers.

POSTSCRIPT

Friends in high places.

'The Speaker of the House of Commons is celebrating the 150th anniversary of the Palace of Westminster with the launch of a limited-edition single malt whisky. It is a century and a half since rebuilding work was completed on the iconic building, following a devastating fire in 1834.

To celebrate this milestone, Sir Lindsay Hoyle, the 158th Speaker of the House of Commons, has selected 'Point of Order' – a 23-year-old scotch – with the help of Chief Whips from the four main political parties.

Artfully matured in a traditional European oak Sherry cask by Murray McDavid, the single malt was created at the Glentauchers Distillery, which has been producing whisky in the Highlands since the late 1800s.

A beautifully balanced whisky with aromas of vanilla fudge and fruit cake, 'Point of Order' boasts sweet spices on the palate and a finish of chocolate and nuts. Sir Lindsay said the special edition whisky would make 'a very special gift for someone who loves the Palace of Westminster'.

'To commemorate our 150th anniversary, there are only 150 bottles available of this limited-edition single malt, which whisky-lovers can bring out on special occasions or keep as an investment for the future' (* see below) he said. 'I am very proud to be celebrating this moment in time with the launch of this magnificent whisky.'

Named 'Point of Order' after the appeals that are made to the Speaker for clarification or a ruling on a matter of procedure in the House of Commons, this unique single malt retails at £200 and is available for sale from the House of Commons shop online and other gift shops on the estate.'

Whisky Intelligence Online 14 December 2020.

(*) I leave it to the reader to ascertain the probability of me heeding the advice to keep a bottle of this unopened 'as an investment for the future'. *Carpe diem quam minimum credula postero.* Translated as: 'Pluck the day, trusting as little as possible in the next one.' Horace, *Odes* (1.ii). But then again …

Some of Our Merv's handiwork

ADMIRING THE VIEW

Ever since Darwin's revolutionary notions on the origin of species, theories of evolution have been used to explain our natural world based on empirical principles. But do they always prove convincing beyond doubt over a more divine authority? GF examines issues of science versus faith based on his own personal quest for answers.

For some years before I relocated from my native Black Country to the Celtic borderlands my family and I occupied a bungalow on the corner of a road leading into a quiet cul-de sac. Our front garden was thus open on two sides and extended to the extent that my late stepfather, considered more as a friend who happened to marry my widowed mother, enjoyed ample scope for his enviable green-fingered talents. One year I counted 86 floral features including hanging baskets; and when I say hanging baskets these monsters trailed five feet to the ground before bouncing along the flagstones. Amazing under any circumstances, the more so that he was severely visually impaired and could barely see what he was doing. Hence every summer I would take a wide-angled photo of this riot of colour and hand it to him with a magnifying glass. Sadly he's long deceased so I recount this both with great affection and in explanation as to why he may have missed certain events going on directly outside his domain.

He didn't always notice, for example, that with a regularity of about four times a year a group of people, sombrely attired in dark clothing, gathered at the junction and huddled conspiratorially as they planned their lines of approach before knocking on doors. They were members of the Church of Jesus Christ of the Latter Day Saints, or Mormons.

Over the years that they had been a'knocking these devotees had come to know that I was not persuaded but equally they knew I was not going to impolitely slam the door in their faces and we enjoyed many a chat on all manner of subjects before, with a cheery wave, they would say goodbye until next time. On this one occasion I was sitting unseen at the rear of the garden when a lady, who was evidently a newcomer to their entourage, gazed at the vibrant display courtesy of Our Merv, as he was fondly known, and declared loudly to her colleagues along the cul-de-sac: 'Oh. Isn't this a wonderful example of the work of the hand of God'. At which point, popping up from behind a large water-butt like an emergent mole dazzled by the brightness, Our Merv declared: 'I think I might have had something to do with it, missus'.

Recorded 15 October 2020

The peels of laughter must have been audible several streets away as the team took time off from their Saviour's work to take a coffee break, in complete absence of any talk of religion.

And that, in my ignorance, is about as germane an example of religious tolerance in the UK as I can relate. There are, we know, countries that demand a far more hard-line adherence but here in good ol' Blighty we are not one of them and the populace is generally free to pursue their particular beliefs when, how, and to what degree or not at all. It's all very personal, all very subjective and all, I would submit, as it should be. One may be devoted, agnostic, atheist or indifferent to all of the above and there is a socially acceptable scope for ambivalence. The licensee of an Inn I frequented at the time was ostensibly so anti-religion that he refused any group to make collections or express their faith on his grounds. Except, for reasons best known to himself, the Salvation Army whom he welcomed with open arms to sell their magazines. *'They do a lot of good'* was his explanation, the implication being that the others didn't. Curious.

My own journey towards an opinion has been convoluted and I have oft struggled to rationalise exactly what that opinion is. Not so much as in a conflict of faith, more one of seeking a line that satisfied my quest for some sort of truth simultaneous with offering an explanation that satisfied my need to know it. My education in the sciences instilled in me the principles of rational explanation yet all set against a backdrop of suspicion that there may be something more. I even explored a few options, from classic Christianity and Buddhism to contemporary pseudoscientific Intelligent Design but, with due respect to them all, none hit my sweet spot and I continued my search.

Fortuitously the most persuasive option was presented to me by nature itself in consequence of the ageing process. Although also attributed to Christopher Bullock's 1716 *The Cobbler of Preston* and Daniel Defoe's 1726 *The Political History of the Devil* it is Benjamin Franklin who in his 1789 letter to Jean-Baptiste Le Roy is best associated with the declaration: 'In this world nothing can be said to be certain, except death and taxes.'

As we begrudgingly pay the one and inexorably head towards the other we all grow older and we all choose to navigate the route in our own way. For me it was the slow-burning recognition – looking back it had been gestating for many years – that the works of the great thinkers may offer some illumination.

So, as I have mentioned elsewhere in my maunderings thus please forgive me for doing so again here, I have of late elected to familiarise myself with the thoughts of the philosophers. There's a lot of them so there's a remaining lifetime of work for me to even scratch the surface, but I am already impressed by those who maintain a contiguous line of reasoning without the need to introduce the concept of a God to bridge conceptual gaps. My investigations are little more than the self-edification of a mere *dilettante*, but they have already aided me greatly in my comprehension, or at least how to go about the attempt.

In the western world a secular approach to thinking branched off around the age of enlightenment. Many eastern traditions continue to interweave philosophy with their religion; secular philosophy is based on that of the ancient Greeks who developed logic as an independent discipline not reliant on insight, scripture or authority. As Julian Baggini, Academic Director of the Royal Institute of Philosophy, describes it: 'God may or may not be dead but for the purpose of acquiring knowledge he is redundant. The human mind works without supernatural assistance to deliver an understanding of the world and ourselves.'

Whist all belief systems should be argued on equal merit in understanding widely diverse cultures, even if we disagree with their tenets, I find it unconvincing to develop strands of coherent thought that are then held together by the glue of dubious deities, the existence of which, by definition, cannot be proven. Hence my leaning toward two towering modern thinkers, Bertrand Russell and Ludwig Wittgenstein. The former was the latter's mentor and their combined reasoning has helped quelled my doubts of a lifetime. Let me take a closer look at my new-found friends.

In 1921 Ludwig Josef Johann Wittgenstein (1889–1951) presented a PhD thesis that was described by his assessor as 'a work of pure genius'. The subject of this glowing epithet was his remarkable *Tractatus Logico-Philosophicus*. Russell wrote the introduction to Tractatus before he and Wittgenstein developed differences of opinion, to the detriment of their friendship.

Wittgenstein concluded that the *Tractatus* had resolved all philosophical problems and he retired from philosophy for many years until realising he had more to offer. His subsequent *Philosphical Investigations*, in which he recanted many of his own earlier assertions in *Tractatus*, did not appear in print until two years after his death.

But back to *Tractatus* which, at just seventy-five pages is considered one of the purest distillations of thought ever written. A central tenet is his assertion: *Wovon man nicht sprechen kann, darüber muß man schweigen.* Whereof one cannot speak, thereof one must be silent.

In essence he is saying that facts and logic are exactly so and can be described; anything beyond these – religion, ethics, aesthetics, the mystical – cannot be rationally discussed and instead require the invocation of feelings, emotions or experiences. They are not *per se* nonsensical, but any statement about them must be, because they cannot be proved or disproved. This view was concurred by Russell who wrote: 'I do not pretend to be able to prove that there is no God. I equally cannot prove that Satan is a fiction. The Christian god may exist; so may the gods of Olympus, or of ancient Egypt, or of Babylon. But no one of these hypotheses is more probable than any other: they lie outside the region of even probable knowledge, and therefore there is no reason to consider any of them.'

Et voilà, no need for me to ponder my deity any further; two minds far finer than mine have done the job for me.

Which brings me in a neat sequitur to a recent knock on my door and my annual visit from our local Jehovah's Witnesses. As with the Mormons at my last place we have discussed the issues many times and I suspect they just give it a try to see if I may have changed my mind.

In the light of my recent acquaintance with Russell and Wittgenstein one would imagine my answer would be even more emphatic. But this time it was different and served to rekindle a confusion that indicated I may still have some way to go. I'll describe the circumstances and invite you to judge for yourself.

Chatting with me on the step stood the usual two callers; charming, unassuming yet evidently fervent in their beliefs. Glancing over their shoulders, with the early sun drenching my home from a cobalt blue sky dotted with cotton wool clouds, across the valley I noticed the Black Mountains draped in a mist that was slowly burning away revealing a scenery that has barely changed in centuries; the River Wye carving its way lazily through the verdant greenery as it brushed past the abandoned castle whose walls could tell a thousand years of tales. A peppercorn dotting of farms concealing the secret lives of their occupants, animals grazing contentedly and, bar for their distant moo-ing and baa-ing, all bathed in near-silence.

Having accepted in good humour that their efforts were still to no avail they turned and departed. Yet as the metal gate clattered shut behind them I could not but avoid admiring their devotion to a faith that caused me to question, just for a moment, whether that imposing panorama that I was gazing on really was purely down to some cosmic chance, a big bang, an alignment of molecules, a roll of the evolutionary dice. Perhaps here, on this glorious morning, and just as in Our Merv's garden all those years ago, there were inscrutable indications of an unfathomable Holiness, a deity at play, indeed, as the lady said, the work of the hand of God. And I reckon, in that moment, I had taken one small step on my own journey towards understanding.

POSTSCRIPT

Live and let live? Now this, I find disturbing. From *BBC Online* dated 24 November 2020:

'Russian police have raided the Jehovah's Witnesses nationwide and made arrests in a new criminal case against the banned Christian-based group.'

In 2017 Russia's Supreme Court banned the Jehovah's Witnesses as 'extremist'. According to the SK (The Investigative Committee) the Moscow group 'studied religious literature … propagandising Jehovah's Witnesses teachings'. It said they 'indoctrinated and recruited new members among the capital's residents and in other regions, to participate in the banned religious movement'. Russian Jehovah's Witnesses claim the State has tortured them and dozens of the faith's followers are being prosecuted in Russia for practising their religion.

In July 2020 the UK government voiced concern about Russia's crackdown on Jehovah's Witnesses, saying the state had 'criminalised the peaceful worship of 175,000 Russian citizens and contravened the right to religious freedom that is enshrined in the Russian constitution'.

In December 2018 Russian President Vladimir Putin said he could not understand why followers of the religion were being persecuted. (Yet) the Russian Orthodox Church (had) welcomed the ban in 2017. A senior Orthodox cleric, Metropolitan Hilarion, called the Jehovah's Witnesses a 'totalitarian sect' on Russian TV. He said: 'It's hard to deny that these cultists will remain and continue their activity … but at least they'll stop openly claiming to be a Christian faith, in other words, in the market place of existing Christian confessions this product will no longer be on display. And I think that's all for the best. It'll save families, people's lives'.

The Jehovah's Witnesses were founded in the US in the late nineteenth century and stick to a very literal reading of the Bible, rejecting the interpretations of many Christian scholars and the Christian doctrine of the Trinity. They believe that the final battle between good and evil will happen soon. They are also pacifists, carry out door-to-door preaching and oppose blood transfusions.

Opposite: view over the Wye Valley and the Black Mountains

This stunning picture was taken by a young man 'in the zone'.

NEGATIVE TO POSITIVE

As self-styled 'spiritual pilgrim' Beth Bruno declares: 'When we judge others, we dim our own light. And the world needs more light right now.' But how and why do we judge others on that scantest of information provided by initial appearances. And is that venerable adage 'you only get one chance to make a first impression' still relevant in the age of social media?

In a novel twist on a hackneyed expression, vocalist Martin Fry of ABC sang on their 1982 hit *The Look of Love*: 'If you judge a book by the cover. Then you judge the look by the lover. I hope you'll soon recover.'

No, me neither, but I suppose it offers an *aide-mémoire* reinforced by a catchy tune that one should not judge others by appearances. Gosh, at fifteen stones in weight, bearded with long hair, ear ring and tattoo and usually clad in leathers or denim, I can tell you all about that one. Yet behind this dishevelled middle-aged monument to excess once lay a youthful athlete of some modest ability and I have dined out on numerous occasions by relating the absolutely true tale of my not-so Grand Participation – I completed the course in an unremarkable time and was left shattered for some while afterwards – at the 1983 Heart of England marathon around the delightful little market town of Atherstone, Warwickshire.

As we jostled for space awaiting the starter's signal I glanced at my fellow competitors, a mixed bunch if ever there was. To my right I saw the scruffiest of urchins in threadbare attire and a battered old pair of what we used to call 'tennis pumps' on his feet. I watched in amazement as he took a black plastic bin-liner and ripped three pieces out of it to accommodate his arms and head. Dressing himself thus he looked, to be frank, quite ridiculous but remained oblivious to anyone noticing. And to my left? Adidas Man. Head to toe designer running outfit. I watched in curiosity as he lifted his wrist and adjusted what appeared to be a watch but from which was emanating a strident 'beep beep beep'. 'What's that?' I enquired. 'Ah', he explained enthusiastically 'set this to what pace you want to run and then just match the beeps to your rhythm. If I set it to around seven minutes per mile to start off then pick up the pace towards the end I should do the course in sub-three hours'. Impressive. There is such a thing as out-psyching your fellows and if anyone was going to do so then here he stood.

Off we went as we steadied to our own tempos. Nowadays anyone running around the block seems to be carrying a water bottle but back in '83 the first hydration station did not appear until ten miles into the race. The next big hurdle to face is what runners refer to as 'the wall', a sudden fatigue at around eighteen miles when the body has exhausted its supply of glycogen in the liver and muscles. It's a horrible feeling, alleviated greatly by those glucose tablets stashed in the back pocket. Anyway, as I hit my own wall who should come dashing past me with a cheery 'hello' but Bin-Liner Man. I never saw him again, he was gone into the distance. At precisely that point I recall coming down a long open slope where, about half a mile yonder, I could see blue flashing lights and a horizontal body being lifted onto a stretcher. By the time I had reached the scene the patient had been covered in one of those silver space blankets before being taken to hospital, so I could not see who it was. But I could distinctly hear a steady 'beep beep beep' going, I would guess, at about seven minutes a mile. And that, as if anyone needed a lesson, was affirmation of not to judge by appearances.

So, let me fast-forward almost four decades to a recent experience where my disinclination to assess by looks alone was challenged but, I am delighted to relate, was not found wanting. Allow me to paint the scene. For reasons that will become apparent when I describe him the young man in question is considered vulnerable so I will do nothing to identify him by name or location or the precise circumstances, but that is all of no relevance to the tale anyway so here goes.

For some considerable time I have been associated with a facility that caters for those unfortunates who, quite simply, cannot be accommodated within the confines of contemporary mainstream education. There are those who might write them off as beyond meaningful assistance. But this is as erroneous as it is judgemental and with careful but intensive nurturing it is astonishing what the human spirit can overcome when played to its strengths rather than disparaged for its weaknesses.

A few years back, for example, I was shown two identically shaped glass tumblers by a man supervising a young lad who had been all but abandoned by the conventional establishment and with evident difficulties, sitting at a diamond cutting wheel. The one glass was etched carelessly with meaningless scratches, the other was a fine piece of hand cut crystal that would have graced any shop. The supervisor handed them both to me, incredulous. 'Six weeks from one to the other' he said in amazement. 'Acquiring that level of skill usually takes years'.

Meanwhile, back to my latest caper and a call I received from another supervisor at the same facility inviting me to be the subject of a photo-shoot for a young photographer wishing to expand his portfolio. I was introduced to a man in his twenties; ascetically thin, maybe standing less than five and a half feet in his boots, cheek studs, tattoos a-plenty and a Mohican haircut. It transpires that he had half of his innards missing and was fed on a liquid diet via a tube in his chest. As if that wasn't enough to spoil his day – and please don't even get me started on the existence of a munificent God who sits atop such things – he was on the upper register of the autistic scale. He was one of the most charming and affable young men I have ever met.

The problems he had to face just to get through the day are simply unimaginable to the likes of most of us. But then, put a Nikon in his hands and wow! Was he in the zone! A shot here, an instruction there, a direction to change stance or shift position, he was totally gone. He compiled a suite of shots, some of which made their way into my inbox shortly afterwards. I immediately took one, blew it up and sent it to a picture framer for hanging in my office. I told his supervisor what I had done and was informed: 'He is dancing round the yard outside with joy'.

Tears rolled down my cheeks for some while afterwards. Yet I go back to the young man who was first presented to me and wonder how many of us would have walked by on the other side. Perhaps, and I am ashamed to even think so, I could have been one of them. But how, in a supposedly advanced society, do we make such discriminatory initial judgements and, perhaps more importantly, why? It appears that genetics and heredities may play an equal role to simple prejudice and behavioural patterns.

In his scholarly book *Interaction of Colour*, first published in the 1960s and still in print, theorist and lecturer Josef Albers, who described himself as 'a martyr to modernism', expanded the ways in which colours are used and perceived in art, architecture, textiles, interior design, graphic media and technology. The book is a standard text for my 'other half' Mary, herself a recognised authority on the use of colours in mapmaking, and I would never have imagined that an artistic reference work would have aided me in one of my own existential dilemmas, but hey-ho life is full of surprises.

Here's a brief extract of what Albers proposed: 'In visual perception a colour is almost never seen as it really is – as it physically is. In order to use colour effectively it is necessary to recognise that colour deceives continually. First, it should be learned that one and the same colour evokes innumerable readings. Instead of mechanically applying or merely implying laws and rules of colour harmony distinct colour effects are produced – through recognition of the interaction of colour – by making, for instance, two very different colours look alike or nearly alike.'

And so, I would submit, by extension does this also apply to physical appearances that, through a similar recognition of the interaction of colour – although I confess I have yet to comprehend precisely what this interaction is – can render two very different identities look alike; or nearly alike.

An analysis posted on her online blog by self-styled 'spiritual pilgrim' Beth Bruno, of South Carolina, USA suggests our perceptions of others are definable by categories underpinned by – you're probably ahead of me in guessing this one – social media.

'People are eager to give their opinions about our lives and choices' she claims. And again by extension in my interpretation, appearances too. 'Sarcastic and rude comments on others' posts seems to bring a sense of satisfaction to our egos. While this may seem innocuous enough (since we can do this with a measure of anonymity) it is far from being harmless to ourselves and others' she concludes. That not only seems reasonable it also brings nastiness and prejudice squarely into the age of cyberspace.

But why are we so quick to judge? According to an article in Psychology Today of May 2018 written by one Elizabeth Dorrance Hall PhD: 'Our brains are attempting to make sense of why people do the things they do. We make snap judgements about people because it moves us on to the next thing our brains need to work out. In other words, it is the quickest way to answer the question: 'What the hell...?' when we see someone do something that makes no sense or evokes a visceral response of anger or aversion'.

Dr Hall goes on to suggest that if we checked ourselves throughout the day to see how often we were being judgemental, we might be shocked by the degree of negative judgement on both ourselves and of others. She advises in conclusion: 'There is a way to flip the habit on its head and if we are willing to change this paradigm we might find that the world opens up for us'.

I fear I may be entering uncharted waters here so to avoid any pretence of psycho-speak I will leave the last word to that anonymous young photographer friend to whom I was delighted to offer a bit of empathy and support that took but a few minutes of a day that I might otherwise have squandered anyway. The thoughts of him 'dancing round the yard outside with joy' are still with me. And, I have to say, I feel rather good about myself. Thus my understanding of the practical consequences of positive changes to that paradigm. Which, I am happy to confirm, are singularly uplifting.

POSTSCRIPT

A few pithy comments of the famous and the not-so:

'Please don't judge people. You don't know what it took someone to get out of bed, look and feel as presentable as possible and face the day. You never truly know the struggles of others'. *Karen Salmansohn*, self-help book author and award-winning designer.

'The least amount of judging we can do the better off we are'. *Michael J Fox*, b. 1961, actor (*Back to the Future* franchise) and latterly advocate for research into Parkinson's Disease, with which he was diagnosed in his 20s.

'Not judging people is the fastest way to peace.' *Jonathan Jackson*, actor, musician and author.

'Do not be the judge of people; do not make assumptions about others. A person is destroyed by holding judgements about others.' *Gautam Buddha*.

'If you judge people you have no time to love them.' *Mother Teresa*.

'When we judge or criticise another person, it says nothing about that person; it merely says something about our own need to be critical.' *Winston Churchill*

ELECTION 2021 FINAL SEATS

Party	Seats
SNP	64
CONS	31
LAB	22
GREENS	8
LIB DEMS	4

Legend:
- SNP
- CONSERVATIVES
- LABOUR
- LIB DEMS
- GREENS

COLOURS OF POWER

Rousing, rebellious, rumbustious; contentious combative and compelling. The USA Presidential Elections of 2020 have redefined politics in an unprecedented polarisation of opinion that may have ramifications way beyond the Land of The Free. But have they also sent us on a path that may change the course of democracy as we know it? And can we apply the brakes?

In the interests of impartiality I generally avoid expressing political *opinion*. But political *commentary*, well, that's fair game and there can be no doubt that the campaigns of the two principal protagonists in the USA Presidential Election of 2020 will offer observers of the unconventional, confrontational and just plain bizarre a voluminous compendium of analysis for decades to come. From the hustings to television debates, speeches and rallies, the final stages will be remembered not so much for soberly considered appeals to the electorate, which were few, but for the intensity of undisciplined argument, wild accusations and sheer vitriol exchanged between the protagonists Messrs Trump the incumbent, and Biden the challenger.

Particularly memorable will be that first televised debate, or more accurately shouting match, during which a bemused moderator sat impotently as two heavyweights verbally slogged it out without either barely getting a constructive word in edgeways. The entire world's media was universally critical. As *The Times* in the UK wrote next day: 'The clearest loser from the first presidential debate between Donald Trump and Joe Biden was America.' It went on to say the event 'was not a debate in any meaningful sense' but rather 'an ill-tempered and at times incomprehensible squabble between two angry septuagenarians who palpably loathe each other'. *The Guardian* described it as a 'national humiliation'.

And yet it continued; in the farrago of the post-election count, a consequence of ballots being conducted under what many believe to be anachronistic provisions by individual States rather than overarching Federal procedures, American comedian Rich Hall offered a spoof analysis comparing a 'soft and cuddly Uncle Joe Biden, who wants to hug the world, with the desperado Trump who was determined to destroy it, probably with the Covid-19 virus'. I cannot recall his exact words but they went along the lines of: 'Not so long ago we had to go abroad to find our tyrants, Gadaffi in Libya, Osama Bin Laden in Afghanistan. Now they are home grown, all you have to do is walk down

Pennsylvania Avenue and there's one staring at you out of the window at number 1600'. The next day, amidst conflicting cries of 'Stop the count' and 'Count those votes' UK comedian Steve Punt wittily observed how this must be the only time in history that people have taken to the streets to demand less democracy. All romping knockabout stuff that had me close to rolling on the floor with laughter.

Rich Hall's *US Election Breakdown*, and Steve Punt's *The Now Show*, both broadcast on Radio 4 were sharp, incisive and rib-achingly funny yet, being the nature of satire, I couldn't help feeling they had accurately articulated the choice faced by the voters. Rarely in the history of Western politics has such an irreconcilable disunity polarised an entire nation. Consensus, cooperation and empathy are concepts that our grandchildren may be studying in their history books.

The implications for world order are profound and it is no great step from imagination to reality in seeing the likes of Russia's Putin, China's Xi Jinping, North Korea's Kim Jong-un and other bastions of a not-so free world rubbing their hands with glee in front of an entrapped populace to gloat: 'Aren't you just glad you haven't got this'. A spectacular own goal by the West.

I was greatly puzzled by it all and have tried to comprehend the sorry morass into which USA politics have been sucked. Regular listeners to my deliberations will know that I have of late taken to looking to the great thinkers for guidance along the path of insight, even if that insight may be only to help explain my own perplexities.

So, it was by coincidence that shortly after Rich Hall's uproarious diatribe, when my ribs were still recovering, that I decided to help my laughter-glands get back to their normal setting by returning my attentions to an article I have been working on. It is the day job, after all. The subject matter is a group of thinkers from nearly a century ago, and as I re-focussed my concentration on them, I was struck by how their venerable institution offered me not a definitive answer, but at least a line of reasoning that satisfied my search for a hook on which I could hang some sort of meaning to contemporary events.

As usual I add the caveat that I am merely an enthusiast who claims no intellectual merit; my exercises are nothing more than my way of soothing Poirot's little grey cells in attempting to reconcile the madness – and I believe the word is accurate in this context – that has unfurled across the pond.

The group in question is the Vienna Circle and they were radical with a capital R. Coalescing in the early 1920s from the 'First Vienna Circle' that had met for several years in various Viennese coffee houses, hence the name, the newer group extended its catchment of luminaries from the worlds of natural, social, scientific, mathematical and analytical philosophy. They met regularly between 1924 and 1936 at the University of Vienna. Following the rise of Nazism many members were forced to emigrate and the murder of their Chairman in 1936 sealed its demise. Nevertheless the Vienna Circle's influence remains immense to this day.

The essence of their radicalism was a complete re-evaluation of empiricism – the establishing of facts by experimentation and observation – by an interpretation of advances in science, based on mathematical concepts. In other words, if it couldn't be proven it was meaningless. This was encompassed in the theory of Logical Positivism, later called Logical Empiricism, the principle of which is sufficiently unpretentious for me to have a stab at elucidating it.

For example, around 1803-04 the idealist Georg Wilhelm Friedrich Hegel declared: 'The spoken word unites the objectivity of the corporeal sign with the subjectivity of gesture, the articulation of the latter with the self-awareness of the former'. Phew.

Now there are those who would say 'gosh, that sounds clever this bloke may be onto something. Let's take a look'. Not so the Circle who attested what patently throwaway guff this all was. Why? Because it cannot be proven and if it cannot be proven or disproven then there is no point in discussing it. Herein was the group's radicalism, a dismissal of ethics, morality, deities, emotions, beauty, empathy and anything else unprovable as to be unworthy of further deliberation. 'There is a sun in the sky'. Fact; look up, there it is. 'There is a God up there'. Unprovable. Thus though the statement may be of singular significance to the faithful it is meaningless to the logician.

To illustrate further let us imagine I owe my business partner some money that I haven't repaid him by the date promised. I have the money, his and my bank accounts confirm the transaction and the calendar shows the due date is passed. Fact. He confronts me in a tirade of expletives and says I will rot in hell. Rot in hell? Where's that, exactly? And there's the crux; all subjective, but as for logical intervention he might as well be shouting 'Yah boo sucks' at me. Yet this is not to say that I am not upset; heated words and deeds can be very emotive and unsettling.

Or empowering, depending on the circumstances. Politicians rank amongst those adept in recognising this and deploying it in their rhetoric to fire up their audiences. Others include Trade Union leaders, motivational speakers and a plethora of activists. Think of Malcolm X, Tariq Ali, Martin Luther King, Nelson Mandela, the list is endless of those who, whether by natural aptitude or formal training, utilise these techniques to impressive effect.

Logical positivism was influenced by many other great thinkers, notably Albert Einstein and Bertrand Russell. Einstein has passed into perpetuity for his work on relativity. Russell's efforts to express logic as mathematics led to some remarkable publications including *The Principles of Mathematics*, a 1903 book in which he argued that mathematics and logics are identical. Although attracting criticism for reasons that I could never begin to understand, much of his subsequent work, amazingly, continues to find practical applications in computer science and information technology.

But how does this relate to my greater comprehension of the Trump–Biden dilemma? Well let's take a closer look at those recent exchanges. Rhetoric to whip up their audiences – no surprise – bluster, emotions, accusations a'plenty. But relatively bereft of verifiable fact. I'll go one further in reminding myself that Mr T in particular has been accused of peddling blatant untruths masquerading as facts.

Thus we enjoy the unedifying spectacle of a public asked to choose the next leader of the free world largely on a combination of emotion, faith, belief, feelings and impression. All powerful stuff that has galvanised widely divergent opinion, but fatuous except as an to appeal to the perceptions. I submit that in the interest of our democracy this cannot be considered best practise. But it does help explain to me the events unfurling before my eyes.

This is not something that is going to be rectified overnight. But I reckon we could make a start by insisting our future potential leaders first demonstrate that they are competent in maturely debating imponderable questions of values, ethics, morality and aspirations – that is a politician's role, after all – yet underpinned with verifiable facts to the satisfaction of an electorate who would be better informed about those who seek to lead us. Whilst there are those who would counter me that we already have such as system in place, I am not persuaded our current process is fit for purpose. Why not? Because we have slowly but surely abandoned our sense of values on the journey between the price of power and power at any price.

It has long been my belief that the answer to maintaining the civility that elevates us above the bear pit lies in an education instilled from the earliest age. Hence my optimism in a 2017 report I happened across recently by Dr Nadia Siddiqui of Durham University's School of Education that seems to support my standpoint. *The Philosophy for Children in Primary Schools* initiative is aimed at developing children's non-cognitive abilities such as communication, self-confidence, fairness and empathy. 'These are deemed to have a

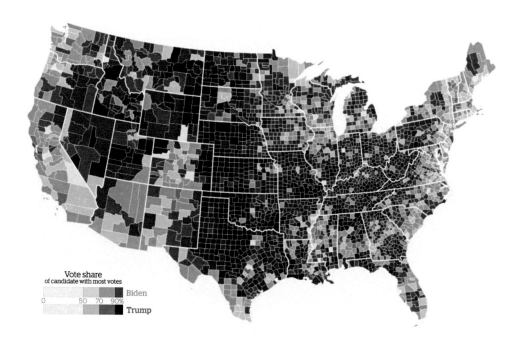

United States presidential election results by county 2020

strong association with outcomes such as attainment and success in later life' Dr Siddiqui says. 'We found the programme had promising effects in improving children's social and communication skills, team work, resilience and ability to empathise with others'.

A little too late, I fear, for our current crop of leaders to benefit from but if we are to arrest the debilitating slide of standards in politics then USA 2020 offers ample evidence that now may be the time to take the longer view. The freedoms of the western world, which we have for too long taken for granted, may depend upon it.

POSTSCRIPT

On the afternoon of the same day this podcast had been recorded in the morning it was confirmed that Joe Biden had secured sufficient electoral college votes to be voted POTUS-elect (President Of The United States.) President Donald Trump, who was playing golf at the time, refused to concede and continued to threaten legal actions based on unfounded allegations of fraudulent election practises.

A few hours afterwards Joe Biden gave his first speech since being declared the winner in which his opening comments included the words: 'I pledge to be a President who seeks not to divide, but to unify; who doesn't see red states and blue states, only sees the United States.'

He also reached out to Trump supporters directly: 'It's time to put away the harsh rhetoric, lower the temperature, see each other again, listen to each other again' Mr Biden said, without mentioning his rival: 'And to make progress, we have to stop treating our opponents as enemies.'

Anthony Zurcher, North America reporter for the BBC, commented: 'As Saturday night's speech demonstrated, at the very least, the Biden presidency will mark a change in presidential rhetoric. The American people have a President-elect who talks about bringing the country together; about being a leader for all the people. Saying it is the easy part; now he has to do it.'

Whilst there are those supporters who would still follow him down the barrel of a canon, and amidst much evidence of what might be considered 'good aspects' of his tenure, former President Donald Trump has, by universal reckoning, cast accepted protocol to the four winds and has secured his place in history for a multitude of the wrong reasons. His displays of unparalleled conduct are simply too long to comprehensively list here but from the outset he was singularly ill-mannered towards his predecessor Barrack Obama, offensive to other nations and wildly reckless as to the Covid-19 epidemic; many observers blaming him directly for the deaths of thousand of Americans.

But it is his demeanour up to, during and post-election that is most egregious. His proclamations include a blank refusal to accept he lost, unfounded allegations that the election was rigged, refusing to concede (as is customary) and, astonishingly, his claims that the FBI and Department of Justice were conspiring against him. By early December 2020 he had instigated over thirty appeals to declare the result illegal, almost every one of which was rejected. Within days that figure was more than doubled, and rising fast. Trump's response was to warn that 'ballot fraud' could spell the end of the GOP (Grand Old Party, i.e. Republicans).

Jack O'Donnell who once managed a Trump casino in Atlantic City, New Jersey and claims to know the man well said: 'In his mind, he will not have lost. He will never concede. It will always be: It was taken from me.' It is suggestive that the Latin motto on Trump's Scottish coat of arms, which he gained after a lawsuit, can be translated as 'Never Concede'.

The criticism of Donald Trump has been universally coruscating, not least at his damaging the very nature of USA democracy to the extent that the discreet consensus enjoyed by previous Presidents who could at least have discourse with opposition has been replaced with partisan antagonism and irreconcilable lines of division. A further hammer fell with the news on 15 December that US Attorney General William Barr, one of Donald Trump's staunchest allies, announced he would be stepping down before Christmas. Mr Barr's term was due to end on 20 January commensurate with Mr Trump leaving office. Tensions developed between the two after Mr Barr suggested there was no evidence of widespread fraud in November's vote.

Much of this turmoil had already been widely predicted. On 4 November 2020, *The Guardian* carried a piece by Corey Brettschneider headed: 'Don't underestimate the threat to American democracy at this moment' in which he suggests: 'Even if Biden does win and the results are accepted, we will have lived through a moment that showed our democracy is less stable than we assumed.'

On 15 December it was reported *(BBC Online)* that President Trump's hopes of clinging on to power had suffered yet another serious blow when Joe Biden's victory was confirmed by the US electoral college and that President Putin of Russia, who had said he would await until the vote was confirmed, became one of the last world leaders to congratulate him. In a speech in which Mr Biden openly castigated Mr Trump for his attempts to overturn the result he noted how US democracy had been 'pushed, tested and threatened' yet 'proved to be resilient, true and strong' and that now is 'time to turn the page.'

There will be many throughout the free world – and beyond – who will be echoing *Amen* to that. Yet in the interests of balance we must acknowledge those millions of Trump supporters who, long after this election is a footnote, will sorely cogitate for years to come on the travesty of it all. And therein lies the dichotomy.

(see also *Last Word* p132; *Epilogue* p133; *Publisher's final addendum* p135)

Rudolf Carnap

Ludwig Wittgenstein

Alfred J. Ayer

Carl G. Hempel

Herbert Feigl

Moritz Schlick, Chairman

Otto Neurath

Hans Reichenbach

Members of the Vienna Circle

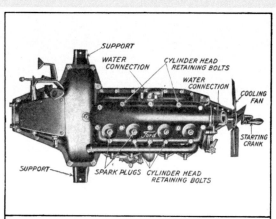

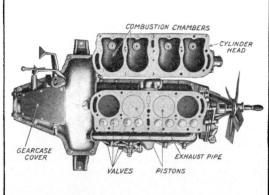

Fig. 12.—Depicting the Distinctive Design of the Ford Motor which Employs a Removable Cylinder Head to Permit Ready Access to the Combustion Chambers, Valves and Piston Parts.

IN LOVING MEMORY

*Within a few years the internal combustion engine,
arguably the most ubiquitous and liberating mechanical
contraption ever invented, is to be outlawed in new cars
and will be consigned to the history books. GF offers an
affectionate reflection on what will be the end of an era.*

The workman levelling the tarmac on the pavement outside my home looked at me with twinkling eyes as I bribed him unashamedly with a four-pack of lager. 'Oh beejabers Sor' he said with a brogue that I suspect was more for effect than authenticity 'Oi'll do that fer yez, so'z I will'. Moments later he was on the driveway as I called out to my mother: 'Remember I always promised you I would sit you in a Roller?' Oh, how we laughed; a long-held promise was fulfilled, albeit not quite in the way my mother expected, as my quasi-Oirish friend posed gleefully for the obligatory photos.

Driving a 'Roller' – that's a Rolls Royce, not the road-flattening variant – is for many car enthusiasts the ultimate in motoring indulgence. It is a fabulous experience; the silk-smooth engine gliding the plot along in a sublime cocoon of comfort where the loudest noise really is the dashboard clock, so unreal as to be surreal. Of course, it doesn't have to be a Roller. My other half prefers Bentleys, Aston Martins and TVRs, none of which are likely to be occupying too much of my workshop space anytime soon but we can all dream.

Ah, the motor car; no-one can remember a time without them being part of our lives. We all have our starting points and I distinctly recall mine being 1962. A mustard-coloured Austin A35 van, registration 3661 FD, allowed my young parents to extend their experiences beyond the range of pedal cycles, buses and trains. The freedom of our car and the open road, with petrol at 3s/6d a gallon (for the uninitiated that's 17.5p) allowed us go where and when we wanted, unfettered by timetables and prescribed routes. I fondly remember as an eight-year-old how I sat on a cushion looking in wonderment out of the rear window as the world sped backwards.

My father became an addict and although we didn't have two pennies to rub together at the time he always found the money to afford a car. He wasn't pretentious by any means. A humble man who left school at fifteen, his car was hardly the mark of a man above his station; it was how he chose to reward himself for his sheer hard graft and determination to get on in life. It was his badge of office.

It is thus no surprise that I should be persuaded by his passion and I, too, have been fortunate to enjoy some lovely automobiles. Although I have appreciated the plush luxury of the big stuff I have long been a devotee of the diminutives and some that I have owned have been amongst the smallest on the road. Not so when I developed my passion for motorcycles and became an adherent of the American philosophy 'It don't mean a thing if it ain't got cubes'. Cubic capacity, that is. And gosh, have I ridden some monsters. Not for speed, more the challenge of handling the beasts. After all, it has long been my maxim that if you have exchanged lots of money for a gleaming machine with enough chrome to cover a small asteroid then the last thing you want to do is drive past people so fast they can't see you. Now that's style.

But, and here's an amazing fact, the A35 van my father bought in the 1960s, the cars he subsequently owned, the fire-breathing behemoths I have ridden all have one thing in common; the four-stroke internal combustion engine. I am unilaterally dismissing the two-stroke expressions; nasty spitting contrivances that may be fine in gardening tools but, for me, have little merit in road vehicles. Or diesel engines; like millions of others I was conned by our Government, yes I stand by the word *conned*, into going diesel by the lure of greater longevity and cheaper fuel only to now being made to feel socially irresponsible every time I fill my tank with particulates.

Then there's the rotary engine, a curious animal if ever. Popularised by the West German NSU RO80 saloon of the 1960s and the Japanese Mazda rotary that featured in several of its sports cars, they were also developed by Norton Motorcycles and raced with some success. As I recall the bike attracted debate as to whether the swept volume of the rotor, depending on how it was measured, amounted to 600 or 1200cc. I rode one once; it was blisteringly crisp but, to me, was no 1200. Then there is the quirkily eccentric Stirling, or external combustion engine. Erm ... I think I'll leave you to look that one up for yourself.

Yet let me not digress with these diversions; the bulk of the world's motor cars have been, and still are, powered by a device that has its roots deep in Victorian times. The materials may have changed, the efficiency improved, the fuel system modified, the emissions lessened, the electrics upgraded, the whole unit controlled by more computing power than put man on the moon but in essence the internal combustion engine in your car is based on a principle first developed by a French engineer, Alphonse Beau de Rochas, following a patent in 1861. Numerous famous names sprang up on the subsequent explosion of car manufacturers; many fell by the wayside but some are still with us from those halcyon times: Mercedes-Benz (1883), Skoda (1895) Renault (1899), Fiat (1899), Cadillac (1901) ... it's quite a list.

From our comfortable leather seat heading at 70 mph along a tarmac motorway we can reflect in bemusement to the time when it was a legal requirement to travel at no more than 4 mph accompanied by someone walking in front carrying a red flag. Though regulations were gradually relaxed, until 1935 you didn't even need a licence to do so.

The four-stroke cycle is also called the Otto cycle, after the German Nicolaus Otto who used spark plugs to fire cylinders in an order of induction, compression, ignition and exhaust. To avoid excess vibration four-cylinder cars have commonly worked on a cylinder-firing sequence of 1-2-4-3 with the up and down movement of the pistons being converted to reciprocal motion of a flywheel via the crank. This is astonishing and worthy of just pausing a moment to reflect that despite advances in nuclear energy, hydrogen fuel cells, solar panels, lithium batteries and a whole raft of wonderful technological advances, that gleaming modern four-wheeled thingy with all the bells and whistles parked in your garage right now is still powered by a device that has remained fundamentally unchanged in over 160 years.

That statistic alone is probably ample justification for why its time is coming to a close. The *dénouement* – the time when new internal combustion engine cars will no longer be available in the UK – was set some months ago at the year 2040; long enough for us all to get used to it. So it came as a jolt to be told this week that it has been brought forward to 2030, with hybrids phased out by 2035. Gosh, that's almost tomorrow.

The internal combustion engine, or at least its incarnation in cars and motorcycles, has in fact been under threat for almost as many years as it has existed. Lobbyists for just about everything from noise, congestion, pollution, anti-social behaviour, industrial relations, road safety – Bridget Driscoll having the distinction of being the first recorded pedestrian to be killed by an automobile in 1896 – even religion and politics, have protested in some way right from the days that Henry Ford declared of his Model T in 1909: 'Any customer can have a car painted any colour that he wants, so long as it is black.' The Model T only came in black so that production line efficiency could be improved. Even in those pioneering days the economics of production were paramount.

Car production has survived the tirades so it is somewhat ironic that its demise has been heralded not so much by humankind's objections but nature's interventions in the way of fossil-fuel depletion, pollution and global warming, none of which were remotely on the horizon back in Henry's prime.

In the meantime, the magnificent motor car has become so ingrained as a fundament of our very existence that, this side of it happening, it is hard to envisage it not being so any more. One investment company newsletter recently described it as Automotive Armageddon. Still, I suppose they said that at the end of the age of steam. But it is disheartening to imagine that from fashion to film – remember the breath-taking car chase featuring Steve McQueen in *Bullitt* that has been reinterpreted numerous times since but never bettered – from functional transport to sumptuous statement of wealth, it will all be no more and there is no question that something indefinable will be lost forever. As for the new order, the prospective concomitant issues of battery manufacture and disposal, charging infrastructure and upgrade of the national grid already disturb me greatly. But they are for another day.

Existing internal combustion cars will survive for many years though I predict they will eventually become the prerogative of enthusiasts much as the aforementioned steam. Traction engines, beam pumps and the Flying Scotsman are now the stuff of legend; perhaps one day you too will find yourself in a museum pointing out to your grandkids what was once your favourite old jalopy.

So I leave the final word to one who has already expressed it all so eloquently. Jeremy Clarkson, formerly of BBC's *Top Gear* until an ignominious fall from grace following his assault on a producer, is nonetheless a talented broadcaster. For the conclusion of the thirteenth series in 2009 he presented a minor masterpiece of emotive prescience, not so much a programme as four minutes of mellifluous artistry.

Picture the scene ... glorious rolling isolated scenery with a single-track road passing not a building nor living soul save for frolicking deer; a gleaming pearlescent silver vehicle of demonically sensuous lines purring around corners and roaring on straights, all accompanied by pacifying music from the maestro of the ethereal, Brian Eno. A pensive Clarkson at the wheel glances towards the camera in tacit acknowledgement. 'Well, it's an Aston Martin Vantage with a V12 engine. So, what do you think it's gonna be like?'

More music, more scenery, more purring and roaring. Clarkson's voice again:

'It is fantastic; it is wonderful, wonderful, wonderful. What it makes me feel, though, is sad. I just can't help thinking that thanks to all sorts of things, the environment, the economy, problems in the Middle East, the relentless war on speed, cars like this will soon be consigned to the history books. I just have this horrible dreadful feeling that what I am driving here is an ending.'

More music, more scenery, more purring and roaring before a clearly wistful Clarkson, in a masterclass of minimalist commentary that left one pondering whether he was closing a series or foreshadowing the end of an era, simply says: 'Goodnight'.

POSTSCRIPT

There is many a cyclist who has been berated by an irate motorist for not paying 'road tax'. Vehicle Excise Duty (VED) or 'car tax' – the confusing term 'road tax' is no longer used officially since the duty is paid on the vehicle not the road – may as well nowadays be called a 'pollution tax' since it is variable depending upon the emissions of the car.

The VED on my vehicle is currently £265 per annum and it goes straight into the general Treasury fund to the tune of, at 2020 prices, around £40 billion. Now, let us imagine a utopia in which every single car owner abandons their car and turns to exclusively using pedal cycles and I'll wager there would be a VED payable on them – probably around £265. Alright, I accept this may be a droll interpretation under poetic licence but the underlying point is a serious one and a feasible alternative could be a road pricing structure. Previous attempts at introducing road pricing were abandoned in the wake of ferocious opposition by motorists so it is ominous to hear of reports that Chancellor Rishi Sunak is revisiting it.

There are other options, but crude taxation hikes would be politically insensitive especially to a Conservative government. I would thus venture with confidence that at this very moment there are mandarins in Whitehall who are exploring increasingly inventive ways to relieve us of our money, and no doubt all done in a sense of civic duty that encourages us how it will be our moral responsibility and the socially acceptable thing to do. Matters are not helped by the coronavirus pandemic and although, at the time of writing, there is great optimism that a vaccine may shortly send it packing, in his budget review before the House of Commons on 25 November 2020 the same Rishi Sunak warned us that 'the economic emergency has only just begun' and could last for many years. That £40 billion VED black hole just has to be plugged somehow.

I am also exercised as to how society itself will respond to the demise of the internal combustion engine. As suggested in the podcast, though manufacture will cease there will still be petrol and diesel cars on the road for years. Scrappage schemes could assist in their removal but it is likely there will still be many in use for some time. So as we get used to the new order in our battery powered vehicles I question whether the zealot fringe – a minority but one that will unquestionably arise; they invariably do – will treat the dwindling petrolheads with similar disdain to those who still choose to wear their old mink coats.

Of even greater concern is that the authorities may 'encourage' scrapping otherwise well-maintained vehicles by punitive and costly sanctions for the most minor infringement of usage or maintenance. Perhaps my imagination is overheating in my sadness at losing such works of art as 'an Aston Martin Vantage with a V12 engine' though, as Winston Churchill said: 'When I look back on all these worries, I remember the story of the old man who said on his deathbed that he had had a lot of trouble in his life, most of which had never happened'. Ah, well; maybe, maybe not. But do please remember you read it here first.

'New research suggests that electric cars have to travel up to 50,000 miles before their carbon footprint falls below that of petrol models. The study, ordered by several manufacturers including Honda and Aston Martin found that making battery packs and other components for electric cars created high levels of greenhouse gas emissions. The report also calls for more investment in renewable fuels to decarbonise petrol and diesel vehicles already on the road.'
The Times Online, 27 November 2020.

'Taxes must increase or services be cut to compensate for the loss of fuel tax income thanks to the advent of electric cars, the Treasury has admitted. Officials have been long concerned about the future loss of more than £30 billion in revenue from drivers. In a new review the Treasury has acknowledged the problem in a way that will spark a debate about how driving should be taxed in the future. One idea would be to charge motorists for every mile they drive. But the AA says such road pricing will be tough to sell politically. Instead, the motoring organisation is proposing a system of 'Road Miles' in which motorists are allowed to drive free of charge for 3000 miles (4000 in rural areas) before they start paying.'
BBC Online 18 December 2020

HOPE
is being able
to see that
there is a
LIGHT
despite all of
the darkness

ONE SMALL WORD

In this intimate reflection GF takes a sideways look at Christmas by focussing on the usage and interpretation of just one associated word that, though comprising only two consonants and two vowels, has ramifications that extend way beyond Christianity and the festive season.

Hanging on the wall at home is an elegant gilt frame, maybe 20 inches high x 15 inches wide, or 51 cm x 38 cm if you prefer, containing a parchment of beautifully illuminated Old School calligraphy that, despite its age, still looks remarkably fresh. Probably because it has been studiously kept out of sunlight and never subjected to extremes of temperature or humidity.

With such cosseting it may be deduced this is something special. It is. Should I now read the opening line: 'If you can keep your head when all about you are losing theirs and blaming it on you' there are no prizes for recognising it as one of the most famous poems in the English Language, Rudyard Kipling's *If*.

The significance of this becomes clearer with the explanation that it was presented to me as a child by my late father with the entreaty: 'Stick by this, son, and you'll do alright'. It has been with me ever since, always on display, never raced or rallied, never abused. Nigh on sity years I have had it now, and though my father has been deceased for over thirty of them, its significance has never diminished.

And so, in a pensive moment recently that found me sitting next to a roaring fire on a dismal December afternoon, I re-read *If* for the umpteenth time and reminisced about dad on a similarly dreary winter day all those years and several houses ago. After decades of suffering he was now, at just fifty-six years old, entering the final stages of the terminal cancer that in hindsight must have been plaguing him anonymously for much of his adult life. He was being looked after at home by a combination of my mother, me and an amazing team of Macmillan Cancer Support nurses.

One might gain the impression this was all purple sad. But it wasn't. In fact there were occasions when we, including the patient, all laughed until our ribs hurt. This is the very blackest of black humour, a distinctive marque that is neither disrespectful nor offensive but is more of a safety valve that allows the participants, including the butt of the humour, to blow off mental steam and carry on under the most appalling of circumstances. The emergency services and armed forces have developed the skill, for that is what it is, to an art form. When dealing with some of the atrocities they face as part of their daily routine there are only two available options; to collapse under the

Recorded 10 December 2020

sheer weight of tragedy or to develop a strategy to cope and continue. Black humour.

So, picture the scene. My father lying flat dozing on a reclining armchair. Suddenly his eyes flicker and he meekly raises a finger to stab heavenwards. 'Quick' said mother 'he feels it's time to go. Get the family round.' The family duly assembled, with dad still feebly pointing, his eyes staring at the ceiling as his lips mouthed words. Tenderly, I put my ear to his mouth: 'What is it dad?' To which he whispered 'Raise me up you pratt, I want a glass of champagne'. Now come on, who amongst us could keep a straight face after that?

Our levity was short-lived and a few days later his oncologist Mr Fairlamb visited us bearing the sad but not unexpected news that nothing more could be done; the end was nigh. With a breath-taking display of pragmatism and sheer dogged determination dad again revisited his 'lift me up' phase, craving more champagne.

The fizz duly opened, the grim entourage stood around dad's recliner, charged flutes in hand, ready to offer the toast. 'Er, what should we say in the circumstances?' enquired mother. To which, without a moment's hesitation, Mr Fairlamb replied: 'We say "Good Health" because whatever the circumstances that is what we all hope for.' And he was right. So we did. The uplift of that simple gesture gave us all the strength to enjoy our most memorable Christmas and New Year together. My father died shortly afterwards.

In recalling this bitter-sweet tale from the comfort of my fireside I glanced at the adjacent bookshelves and noticed a book by comedian Spike Milligan. I am a huge fan so there is a whole row of his books but this one in particular caught my eye; the one in which he loses his beloved wife Patricia 'Paddy' Ridgeway to breast cancer in 1978. She, too, had been visited in her final days by her Doctor. She asked if she was going to die. When Milligan learnt the Doctor had relied 'Yes' he exploded in a tirade of expletives. 'You have taken away her hope' Milligan cries. And there is that word again – hope. Rather like love, hope may not conquer all. But it is evidently a good starting point in the attempt.

My stance on religion is that of ambivalence; whilst I have little interest in pursuing the existence of a deity I respect those that do. So I hold myself accountable to those of faith in my simplistic interpretation of the Christmas message, a time when we celebrate the infant Jesus being delivered to save us from our sins. He was pilloried, excoriated and crucified. Yet at Easter he rose from the grave and took his place in heaven. And herein is the quintessence of Christianity. For us mortals left behind Jesus offered the hope of eternal life.

The word hope is both noun and verb. As the former it describes a *feeling* of expectation or a desire for a particular thing to happen. As a verb it expresses a *desire* for something to happen or be the case. It is usually positive *per se* and even when expressing negative expectations ('he is a horrible man; I hope he gets what he deserves' for example) the desired outcome of the 'hope' as expressed by the 'hoper' is affirmative in its intent. It is a curious or disturbed mindset that routinely hopes for bad tidings to befall one's self, as may be symptomatic of depression or mental illness. Against a contemporary backdrop of widespread conflict and famine, global warming and the Coronavirus pandemic the imperative for universal hope has arguably never been more acute.

From hope emerges faith. This, in the light of its inherent positivity, is hardly surprising that the concept of hope, or at least its equivalent either express or implied, is not confined to Christianity.

In his 2011 book *Paganism*, author Owen Davies writes: 'It is crucial to stress right from the start that until the twentieth century, people did not call themselves Pagans to describe the religion they practised. The notion of Paganism, as it is generally understood today, was created by the early Christian Church. It was a label that Christians applied to others, one of the antitheses that were central to the process of Christian self-definition. As such, throughout history it was generally used in a derogatory sense'.

Yet the Pagan expression of hope is not diametrically opposed to that of Christianity. The guiding Pagan principle 'Do as thou wilt ain harm no other' is a model for harmony, that same harmony which is central to eastern religions harking back to Confucius. Pagan theology is based primarily on experience, with the aim of Pagan ritual being to make contact with the divine in the world that surrounds them. Their hope lies in an unsophisticated expectation that the sun will rise tomorrow and the seasons continue to change. The analogous Druidism – many modern Druids are Pagans – conform to similar tenets of harmony, connection, and reverence for all things and the environment.

The concept of hope permeates world religions and may manifest itself in diverse ways. Remove or suppress the element of hope and the whole edifice crumbles; hope is its sustenance and is to a degree self-perpetuating.

Consider for example, those troubled regions where freedom and liberty are at a premium or even non-existent. Here, hope lies in liberation from the oppressor. In his 2008 book *The Hope of Liberation in World Religions* Editor Miguel A de la Torre collates contributions from scholars across the globe who share the religion or belief systems they describe in order to articulate liberationist concepts from the perspective of those who have been marginalised.

A small word that is often used grammatically incorrectly or dismissed inconsequentially, hope is a fundament of human nature. It has wings that allow us to soar with the eagles in our aspirations for the future, however rooted we may be by words that bring us crashing back to the stark reality of the now.

In an article entitled *In Rescuing the Word 'Hope' and Recovering Its Biblical Meaning* published in Community in Mission dated 11 January 2017 Monseigneur Charles Pope offers eloquent witness:

'Hope, like love, is a word that needs to be rescued from a world that has overused and misused it for so long that its original meaning has been nearly lost. Hope has come to imply more of a vague wish for something. Sometimes it's used as a substitute for the word 'maybe'. For example, if a person says: 'I hope it doesn't rain tomorrow' he likely means 'I wish it wouldn't rain' or 'It'll probably rain but it sure would be nice if it didn't.' Here is another example: If a person is asked 'Will you be at the meeting tomorrow?' and responds, 'I hope so' he probably means 'Maybe I'll be there.'

In both examples doubt surrounds the situation and the desired result seems improbable. While the word hope is not used only in situations like this, too often it merely represents wishing for an unlikely outcome.

I cannot set forth an entire treatise on hope here, but I would like to try to rescue it from its secular meaning, or at least to distinguish the theological virtue of hope from secular hope.

The theological virtue of hope is confident expectation. The theological meaning of the word hope has a much more vigorous quality. The definition of theological hope that I memorized back in Seminary is the older one, which was in use prior to the current Catechism.

Hope is the Theological Virtue wherein one confidently expects God's help in attaining eternal salvation' Msgr Pope concludes.

As Alexander Pope (no relation, that I am aware of) said in his *An Essay on Man* first published in 1734: 'Hope springs eternal'. So it does; even for those, like me, hovering on the fringes of unenlightened ambivalence. This Yuletide I am blessed that my mother, now heading disgracefully towards her 90s, is still with me to enjoy it together on this earth. Yet I hope that one day, with no religious connotations I am conscious of, we might both be reunited with my father in the next. And I confess it may be some time before I fathom the rationale behind that one.

But for now, I hope – with confident expectation – you have a very Merry Christmas and a happy, prosperous and virus-free new year.

POSTSCRIPT

'After another year of difficulty at home and abroad those of us who are Christians will gather to remember once more the birth of a child filled with hope and promise. In churches across America we will join fellow believers all over the world and celebrate the birth of Jesus ... At this special time we note the Christmas message recently offered by the World Council of Churches, which reads in part: 'In the season of advent, Christmas and Epiphany we are particularly aware of God's gift of light ... this is the light that gives us hope for the present world in spite of disunity, abuse, hatred, violence, poverty, greed and corruption. Hope is important in times such as these'. Rev. Dr Chuck Corrie, Director of the Centre for Peace & Spirituality and University Chaplain, Pacific University, writing in *Huffington Post*.

'God never gives someone a gift they are not capable of receiving. If He gives us the gift of Christmas, it is because we all have the ability to understand and receive it.' Pope Francis.

'May you never be too grown up to search the skies on Christmas Eve.' Anon.

I would like to dedicate this episode, and indeed this series of *In My Opinion*, to 'my other half' and publisher Mary Spence MBE in acknowledgement of her constant support and encouragement and in recognition of her suggesting: 'this might be a fitting moment to conclude'. Quite right, Mary, quite right.

Thank you for listening.

IF - Rudyard Kipling

If you can keep your head when all about you
Are losing theirs and blaming it on you,
If you can trust yourself when all men doubt you,
But make allowance for their doubting too;
If you can wait and not be tired by waiting,
Or being lied about, don't deal in lies,
Or being hated, don't give way to hating,
And yet don't look too good, nor talk too wise:

If you can dream - and not make dreams your master;
If you can think - and not make thoughts your aim;
If you can meet with Triumph and Disaster
And treat those two impostors just the same;
If you can bear to hear the truth you've spoken
Twisted by knaves to make a trap for fools,
Or watch the things you gave your life to, broken,
And stoop and build 'em up with worn-out tools:

If you can make one heap of all your winnings
And risk it on one turn of pitch-and-toss,
And lose, and start again at your beginnings
And never breathe a word about your loss;
If you can force your heart and nerve and sinew
To serve your turn long after they are gone,
And so hold on when there is nothing in you
Except the Will which says to them: 'Hold on!'

If you can talk with crowds and keep your virtue,
Or walk with Kings - nor lose the common touch,
If neither foes nor loving friends can hurt you,
If all men count with you, but none too much;
If you can fill the unforgiving minute
With sixty seconds' worth of distance run,
Yours is the Earth and everything that's in it,
And - which is more - you'll be a Man, my son!

LAST WORD

Plus ça change, plus c'est la même chose. An epigram by Jean-Baptiste Alphonse Karr in the January 1849 issue of his journal *Les Guêpes* ('The Wasps'). Literally 'The more it changes, the more it's the same thing.'

It is the settled order that nothing stays the same and so it is the ultimate oxymoron to suggest that we accept the inevitability of change as a *status quo*. However, when I embarked on this series in June 2019 few could have envisaged that within weeks we would be engulfed by events of such enormity and magnitude, all of which were momentous in themselves but each of which was to be overshadowed by one in particular.

Worldwide Black Lives Matter protests, unparalleled levels of political disturbances from Hong Kong to Belarus, alarming accelerations in climate change and species loss, massive cyber-attacks across continents, the baffling behaviour of President Donald Trump; the list is a lengthy one.

Yet all trail in the wake of possibly the most serious issue ever to confront mankind; the Coronavirus pandemic. The story of how the virus broke out, the universal suffering it inflicted and the monumental efforts to develop a vaccine already comprise the stuff of legend. There is a long way to go and as American orator and politician William Jennings Bryan (1860–1925) observed: 'Destiny is not a matter of chance; it is a matter of choice. It is not a thing to be waited for; it is a thing to be acheived.'

Yes, things will continue to change. But the last couple of years or so have been particularly momentous in their scope. By happenstance I was presented with the opportunity to contemporaneously record my observations on some of them alongside more benign matters that confirm how life as we know it still tends to go on.

It is thus rewarding to imagine that one day this book may provide a helpful reference point for students not yet born reflecting on a unique slice of our social history. In the meantime I know that, for all its foibles, I shall continue to be impressed by the sheer indomitability of the human condition.

That was it. Job done. And then, this happened …

EPILOGUE

God bless America.

It is the curse of the writer that betwixt the time of dotting the final full stop on the last paragraph and the finished work appearing in print some element of content will have been overtaken by Harold Macmillan's 'events, dear boy, events'. (*Thoughts on Thoughts*, p71).

So – and here's a trick of the trade, for that is all it is – in an effort to mitigate the effect one may take to a bit of crystal ball-gazing in predicting events that may keep the work current for just that little while longer. It does not require any unique talent of prescience or great leap of soothsaying to see the continuing rise of China and India as world players, the ongoing march of Scottish nationalism, the post-Brexit hangover, the powder keg nestling beneath South Africa, the eventual landing on Mars, the unifying scientific theory of everything ... and so on *ad desperandum* or *optimum* depending on your perspective.

Even so, when I wrote *Last Word* at just about the latest possible moment before proof-reading and despatching the completed work to my publisher, never in my most fevered imaginings could I have envisaged the 'events, dear boy, events', the consequences of which will enshroud us for a long time hence. And which necessitated me re-considering my concluding remarks at the very last moment before my publisher demanded: 'Let's have it, then'.

As indicated in *Colours of Power* (p113) the Presidency of Donald Trump has been, erm ... let me say, remarkable. In the final paragraph of the *Postscript* I suggest: 'in the interests of balance we must acknowledge those millions of Trump supporters who, long after this election is a footnote, will sorely cogitate for years to come on the travesty of it all'.

Just hours later on the morning (UK time) of 7 January 2021 the world awoke to the shocking aftermath of a previous day of unprecedented violence and anarchy in the very heart of USA democracy where hordes of protesters and a representative taxonomy of The Great Unwashed invaded the Capitol Building in Washington DC. As with those who recall JFK being shot in 1963 remembering exactly where they were when it happened, this one is up there. It would be irresponsible of me to let it pass unrecorded.

My gosh, this really was history in the raw; the mish-mash of some primal broth from which we will not be sure what will be supped 'pon the spoon until it cools but which we know will bear little resemblance to what ingredients we lobbed in the pot.

Five people dead, delegates in a fortified concrete citadel hiding behind lecterns as a mob invades, armed security guards brandishing their weapons, violent threats, pipe-bombs, a scene described as 'close to civil war' – awful, simply awful. And painful to watch.

It was a tragedy. As a writer and broadcaster it is not often that I am lost for words. I was lost for words. My golden opportunity; my inadequacies exposed.

I will leave it to others to document these astonishing events but for those 'students not yet born reflecting on a unique slice of our social history' to whom I allude in *Last Word* I place on record that, even as one who does remember where he was when he heard of Kennedy being shot (*About the Author*, p4) I have never witnessed anything more alarming. I would wish that I never have to do so again, but now this particular and hitherto unimaginable line has been crossed I fear I will.

The eyes of the world stared on these unbelievable events; not all of them munificent. Cue back to *Colours of Power* (p113): 'The implications for world order are profound and it is no great step from imagination to reality in seeing the likes of Russia's Putin, China's Xi Jinping, North Korea's Kim Jong-un and other bastions of a not-so free world rubbing their hands with glee in front of an entrapped populace to gloat: 'Aren't you just glad you haven't got this'. A spectacular own goal by the West.'

Prescience? Note to mother: 'Mom, I think this could be your lad's finest hour. Oh, and don't forget to bring the milk'.

Entire forests must have been pulped to accommodate the ensuing copy and for those 'students not yet born' to whom I allude this will be rich pickings. However, in a blizzard of coverage it was one in particular that impressed me. Broadcast on BBC Radio 4's *Point of View* on Sunday 10 January 2021 under the title of *A Turning Point For Democracy* – and, I say with some envy, the excellence of which I strive to emulate – essayist and staff writer for The New Yorker, Adam Gopnik offers a nine-minute exposition to 'make sense of events in Washington and argues the attack on Congress was predictable. And he explores the fascinating mismatch between the cult leader and the occult'.

He does so from his self-confessed alternating perspectives of an 'I told you so' and a 'know-it-all'. Perceptive, analytical and razor-edged in its economy of language yet barely constrained in its controlled anger and wonderment, this was a man who was clearly keeping shock in check whilst maintaining professional restraint. A masterpiece of evaluation suffused with controlled emotion; I commend it to the House.

Yet still, as I note in *One Small Word* (p127), I shall continue to be 'impressed by the sheer indomitability of the human condition'. Perhaps therein lies the essence of my own sense of hope.

Thank you, again, for sharing in my deliberations. And, if you should happen to concur with any of them, thank you for that also.

Now that really is The End. Or perhaps another Beginning. *Plus ça change ...*

— fin —

'History is not there for you to like or dislike. It is there for you to learn from it. And if it offends you, even better. Because then you are less likely to repeat it. It's not yours to erase. It belongs to all of us'. *Lt. Col. Allen Bernard West* retd United States Army (1961-)

Publisher's final addendum: On Wednesday 20th January 2021, and at his third attempt to attain the highest office in the land, Joseph Robinette Biden Jnr. took his oath as the 46th President of the United States of America; the oldest (born 1942) and only the second Catholic (after John F Kennedy).

In part due to the covid pandemic, in part following the aftermath of the shocking events on Capitol Hill exactly two weeks previously, the concourse – that same concourse where in January 2017 a newly inaugurated Trump mendaciously declared his modest assemblage as 'the largest presidential inauguration in history' *(all media)* – was sparse on people but instead filled with hundreds of thousands of flags representing those who could not be there.

One not there through choice was now-former President Donald Trump, the first USA President in history to be impeached twice; for earlier allegation of abuse of power and for his 'incitement to insurrection' on Capitol Hill. He left the White House for the last time in helicopter Marine One to head for Joint Base Andrews a few miles away without greeting his successor. More than 25,000 National Guard troops protected proceedings, a figure estimated by *Dawn* magazine (and others) to be five times the number of US troops currently deployed across the whole of Afghanistan and Iraq combined.

A surreal conclusion to one of the most bizarre presidencies in American history, the new incumbent declared: 'Democracy has prevailed.'

The death toll from the riots on 6th January rose to six when, on the Saturday following the disturbances and in circumstances that his Commander attributed to his state of mind as a 'line of duty casualty', Officer Howard Liebengood, aged fifty-one, died by suicide.

Storming of the United States Capitol in Washington DC on Wednesday 6 January 2021

MUCH OBLIGED . . .

Photographs and images reproduced throughout are the author's own unless acknowledged below.

p10 . . . . archiveatthebbc
. . . . flickr.com

p15 . . . . The Misanthropic Bunny
. . . . iepurelemizantrop.wordpress.com

p16 . . . . British Library
. . . . Shelfmark MS11353, Public Domain

p21 . . . . commons.wikimedia.org
. . . . Charles D P Miller, cc-by-sa-2.0

p28 . . . . thesaurus.plus

p32 . . . . azquotes.com

p33 . . . . omniglot.com

p34 . . . . theguardian.com

p39 . . . . en.wikipedia.org

p40 . . . . commons.wikimedia.org
. . . . Orlando Ferguson 1893, Public Domain

p45 . . . . bostonraremaps.com
. . . . Alexander Gleason 1892

p46 . . . . yuniversity.tumblr.com

p49 . . . . commons.wikimedia.org
. . . . Dirk Ingo Franke, cc-by-sa-3.0

p52 . . . . commons.wikimedia.org
. . . . RCraig09, cc-by-sa-4.0

p63 . . . . bruurcegerencser.net

p64 . . . . commons.wikimedia.org
. . . . Vigneshwar Senthivel, cc-by-sa-4.0

p69 . . . . commons.wikimedia.org
. . . . Ythlev John Jones, cc-by-sa-42.0

p70 . . . . commons.wikimedia.org
. . . . Moritz Nahr, Public Domain

p76 . . . . thunderbirds.fandom.com

p81 . . . . dreamstime.com
. . . . Ilona Lablaika

p82 . . . . commons.wikimedia.org
. The Illustrated Police Budget 1895, Public Domain

p85 . . . . twitter.com
. . . . Simon Singh

p88 . . . . zazzle.co.uk

p94 . . . . archdaily.com

p99 . . . . whizzky.net

p112 . . . . thescottishsun.co.uk

p116 . . . . en.wikipedia.org

p119 . . . . britannica.com
. . . . timetoast.com
. . . . famousfix.com
. . . . alchetron.com
. . . . prabook.com
. . . . en.wikipedia.or

p120 . . . . wikiwand.com

p131 . . . . etsy.com

p126 . . . . dreamstime.com
. . . . noracarol

p135 . . . . commons.wikimedia.org
. . . . TapTheForwardAssist, cc-by-sa-4.0

cover . . . . dreamstime.com
. . . . Aleksandr Stepanov